SURVIVING TO THRIVING

A Practical Guide To Go From Barely Living, To Living With Joy

Including daily take-away tasks to implement into your own life

While every precaution has been taken in the preparation of this book, the publisher assumes no responsibility for errors or omissions, or for damages resulting from the use of the information contained herein.

SURVIVING TO THRIVING - A PRACTICAL GUIDE TO HELP YOU GO FROM BARELY LIVING TO LIVING WITH JOY

First edition. March 1, 2022.

Copyright © 2022 Jane Adams.

ISBN: 978-0473620462

Written by Jane Adams.

Introduction

They say that we all have a day, a dark day when we either sink or swim. I don't think I had a day, but rather a period of time where things were so dark I knew if I didn't change something I would leave my girls without a mother, just as I had been left without mine.

So I survived my dark day of the soul, my dark period. A time when I was suffering from depression, anxiety, adrenal fatigue, I was scared, bone tired and disassociated with my mind and my body

I was so homesick and fearful of where I was living that it physically and mentally hurt

Earthquakes were ravaging my home, the place I should have felt totally safe

I had a toddler and a new-born in tow

To the outside world I was ok but on the inside I was barely hanging on

I had become a very good actress by this point in my life so no-one really knew the battle that was raging inside

I felt totally and completely numb, I couldn't feel otherwise I'd lose it emotionally

I got to the point where something had to be done differently

I didn't enjoy life, I didn't care if I lived but I did care that my girls were safe

That they didn't end up without a mum like I had

So I joined a network marketing company..........

Jane Elizabeth

I dedicate this book to so many people in my life who have always loved me, even when I didn't love myself.

My Mum and Dad (I miss you more than you will ever know and I hope you are looking down on me with pride), my Step Mum Jean and my wonderful Step Sisters, Susan and Pauline and my Step Brother David.

Without any of you I dont think I would have survived any of it.

To my Husband Steve for always loving me despite it all and to my beautiful girls Chloe and Hannah, without you in my life I would have nothing, you are my moon, my stars and will always have my entire heart. I love you x

I hated every minute

I felt like mutton dressed as lamb, like a sleazy salesperson

Pushing myself to do selfies and lives - feeling like an imposter

But........

It was my first step to here

Network marketing is an amazing place to teach you about growth (and it gets such a bad rap unfairly in my opinion)

I began to immerse myself in self-development in a massive way

Learning all I could about the mind and body connection

How my thoughts could either save me or bury me

And then my soul kicked in and a spark was lit, I fed the spark with more and more and the fire was suddenly raging

So I came out of my darkness and into my light

And it led me to here

A place that isn't perfect (but I don't believe anything is)

A place where I am learning more and more every day about loving my mind and my body, confident in my own skin, knowing what I want

Being led by my soul, leaning in to my intuition and feeling brave and powerful for probably the first time in my life

And I am so grateful for the entire journey

Without it I would not be the person I am here, today, in this moment, so I am grateful for every part, the good, the bad and the ugly, and there were so many ugly moment I can't count them

Healing isn't immediate, it's a process, it takes time

But I want you to know that no matter how dark things seems there is always light - find it, trust it and let it lead you

Let this book, my words, my story be the catalyst that you need to change, to become empowered, to build your self-worth, your self-love, to know that it really is possible, let me take your hand and show you the way.

Chapter 1 - The Day Everything Changed

My life changed when I was 7 years old, one minute I was a normal happy go lucky little girl and the next everything changed. My mum had cancer, she'd had cancer for a while but we lived with it, to me it was normal, my life was just normal and I didn't really think anything of the fact that she was ill a lot, was in and out of hospital, had turned yellow – with what I now know was jaundice – it was just all normal, until the day she died.

I remember she was upstairs in bed and my dad was up there with her and the doctor came. My sister Cathy and I must have known something was going on because we sat on the bottom stair together listening for clues, trying to decipher what was happening, two little girls whose worlds were about to be turned upside down.

I heard dad thanking the doctor and then he came downstairs.....or at least I think that's what happened, that is the memory I have carved out for myself, whether it actually happened quite like that I'm not sure, I have erased a lot of that time from my thoughts, I presume as a protection for my emotions, because if I remembered them all they would surely destroy me.

I don't remember Dad crying.... ever, although I am sure he did in secret away from the eyes of his two young impressionable daughters, I don't remember what he said to us, I don't even remember crying myself that day, I'm not sure I knew the severity of what had just happened or how it would affect every single thing about my life from that day forward, how could I, I was seven.

We were never allowed to talk about her again after that, I think for dad to be able to cope with losing his wife and now having a 10 and a 7 year old to deal with, two girls at that, he needed to shut it all out and pretend it had never happened, never talk of it and definitely don't cry. As an adult now I get it, I completely understand why he had to do what he had to do but back then as that small child I was completely and utterly lost.

I remember some days later that he wanted Cathy and I to go to the funeral home to see her, I think he wanted us to see that she was at peace, that she was not yellow anymore, that she was finally free of pain but I didn't want to go, even at that age I think I knew that seeing her like that would not be beneficial, everything in me was crying out not go, to not see her, my intuition was begging me to do what was best for me and to not go. Instead I followed what my dad wanted and I went.

I got up to her feet and I froze, I physically would not walk any further, I could not make my eyes look up any further up to her face and I ran - that is my first memory of crying, of sobbing so hard and for so long that I was exhausted.

That day has never left my memory, countless others have, many things that I should remember I can't, many things that I wish I could remember I don't – but that day, that memory has stuck with me forever and it is as real today as it was then, 40 odd years ago.

It's funny that it was 38 years later that I finally got around to writing this book (yes I have procrastinated over writing it and finishing it for nearly 3 years) as that is how old mum was when she died, 38, such an insignificant number to you no doubt but to me it is a number that I hate. It's a number that I dreaded getting to myself, even as a child I can remember thinking that when I hit age 38 something will happen to me, because that's the age when people leave.

Looking back at it all and the way it all played out we should have had some sort of counselling, but this was England in the 70's and dad was way too proud to ask for help, to admit that we needed help to get through it, you just didn't do that in those days, you struggled through, stiff upper lip and all that - and struggle through we did, struggle through I did for the rest of my life.

I went from a happy go lucky girl surrounded by love and hugs to someone who became reserved almost overnight, starved of love and affection and no understanding of what had just happened. Dad was never the emotional one, he was never the one to give big hugs, to tell us he loved us – that was mum's job and we knew that was just how it was. Dad hadn't really wanted kids, it was mum who did and who persuaded him to have us.

So dad went to work and provided for us and mum stayed at home and loved us.

Don't get me wrong I loved my dad, he was the best person and I was absolutely devastated when he died too not that long ago. But by then we had built many bridges the two of us, I had an adult's perspective to look back at things by, I knew he loved me, and as he got older he found it easier and easier to show me. Oh how I wish he had found it easy 40 years ago.

So on that day and in the days and years that followed mum had gone and physical love, like hugs and kisses, for the most part was gone with her.

On that day I went in to my bubble, a little girl completely lost, utterly despondent, no clue how to cope with what had just happened to her life, becoming more and more introverted, less able to see the world as a nice place to live in. I went in to my own head and I didn't come out of it until many years later.

In fact, I still live there on occasion but nowadays it's become much easier to also live in the real physical world where everyone else resides.

Chapter 2 - I Was The Fat Girl

My battle with food started young, I'd always had a sweet tooth and loved everything that was bad for me. I was bought up in the 70's in England, the time of microwave dinners, angel delight and E numbers. My household was also one where you didn't leave the table until you had eaten everything on your plate – we would sit there, all of us in silence, around the dinner table until each plate was clean regardless of whether we were full or not.

And so I learnt that food was to be eaten, all of it and that other types of food, the good stuff, the sugary stuff that tasted amazing made me feel a little bit better about my life, it gave me comfort, it became the love that I was craving – and so started the emotional eating habits.

I remember talking to dad about my eating habits years later and he said "cake made you happy and so I let you eat it" and eat it I did, way too much of it.

School was a blur of bullying and name calling – thunder thighs, fatty, fat pig, ugly – you name it I was called it all. I hated that time of my life – at this point dad had remarried and I had a step family. How I longed for my step mum to love me the way mum had, I put her on such a pedestal that there was no way she could live up to my expectations. I had step sisters, much older than me, who were bright, bubbly, confident, thin.........so different to me. I had a step brother that I couldn't talk to, I was way too shy and didn't know what to do with boys.

I longed to be like them, all of them, I loved them with all of my heart, both my step mum and my step family but yet at the same time I hated being with them – being with them just showed me what I wasn't and what I would never be, it showed me all my short comings, all my self-hate, my low confidence – it taught me to hate myself and so that's what I did for a very long time.

I was different to them, I was becoming more and more introverted and more and more unhealthy. My step mum, trying to help me, put me on a diet when I was 12. I lost a lot of weight but I hated it, I didn't want to diet, food was my emotional crux and when that was taken away from me my mood and my self-esteem plummeted to an even lower level – yes I was thin now but I was just as desperately unhappy as before.

My image in the mirror however liked being thin, I can remember for the very first time seeing my collar bone and thinking I like the way this looks and years later during the terrible, darkest times when I was gripped by an eating disorder this was what I was striving for, I wanted my collar bone to stick out so much that I wanted it to be the first thing anybody noticed about me, it gave me some sort of power.

The thin phase during those early years did not last long however, none of us ate particularly healthy. One of my step sisters was at this time going through catering college and she would teach me what she was learning and between us we would bake pies and cakes and scones and lemon meringue pie and all sorts of yummy desserts every single weekend. I was good at baking it seemed and people would praise me for it so I wanted to do more of it, I loved pleasing people, I craved love and attention and so baking became kind of my thing.

That became our Sunday afternoons, baking and cooking followed by lots of eating and weight gain. I was momentarily happy, being praised and feeling good about what I was doing but then after I ate the food and put the weight back on I was once again fat, miserable and trapped in a never ending cycle of craving the food, eating the food, berating myself for being so weak and upsetting myself to the point of eating more of the food to make myself feel better.

I want to make one thing really clear here – it was me, it was all me – I was never pressured or bullied into wanting to be thin by my family, they were and still are to this day my biggest cheerleaders, the people I long for when I feel out of sorts, the people I miss the most in the entire world now I have moved away from the UK and live abroad, What I was doing, how I was feeling – that was all on me.

Then on that fateful day when I was about 22 years old I went on a walk up a landmark in Wales called The Great Orm, I had been yoyo dieting for years at this point, always failing and always berating myself for failing – I remember my then brother in law saying that I would never be thin and remain thin if I was just dieting to please other people, that for it to work I had to want to do it for me (he'd been there you see, he was the fat kid too and now he was a black belt karate expert and probably one of the healthiest people I knew). This seemed strange to me because of course I wanted to lose weight, I hated being fat, I was miserable and I honestly hated myself with such a passion that I was my own worst bully.

But on that day, on that walk up that never ending hill I hated my out of control eating and the condition of my body so much I vowed never to over eat again, never to be so out of shape and that no matter what it took I would be thin and suddenly the words he had spoken not long before made complete and utter sense.

I think this, coupled with the fact that I was so lonely, had never had a boyfriend, was completely and utterly alone in my life and all I wanted was someone to love me, spurred me on and made me want to do something about the way I looked. I longed to be loved, I longed to be part of a couple, I longed to have a relationship just for me, someone who wanted me. It had never happened prior to this I told myself because a) I was ugly b) I was fat c) I hated myself, d) who in their right mind would want me………. need I go on…….

And so I got to work – I dieted, I exercised, I learnt a lot about nutrition and what to eat and what not to eat and I lost weight. I remember telling everyone when I get to a size 14 I'll be happy and let up on myself a bit. Then I got to a size 14 and changed that goal posts saying once I am a size 12 I'll be happy, you can obviously guess the rest, it was never enough, it never stopped, I was never thin enough.

In my mind I would get thin, I would suddenly like myself, boys would suddenly like me, I would get married, I would be happy and I would live happily ever after amen.........guess what, none of that came true, life wasn't the love story I had dreamed about, it wasn't one of the romantic comedies I watched over and over again pretending the leading lady was me – life was cruel and it was ugly and it was a never ending barrage of abuse that I was hurling at myself day after day after day. Even thin the bullying never stopped – I still looked in the mirror and saw fat which made me eat less and exercise more every, single, day.

My body was on to me though, it knew I was starving it, it knew that it needed food and so every single bit that I gave it it kept and it stored and it used as fuel to keep my organs alive. I felt that even my body was against me and so weight loss stopped at around a size 10.

So there I was in my 'when I get to a size 8 I'll be happy' state with my body having other ideas and keeping hold of the little it was getting and so that allusive size 8 never materialised. Once again I had failed, why are you so stupid, you fail at everything, you are such a failure, why can't you do anything right, what on earth is wrong with you, no wonder you are alone and nobody loves you ....on and on it went. A viscous cycle of starving, over exercising and bullying myself constantly. My mind was free falling in to despair, I was giving up, I had literally had enough.

Chapter 3 - The Power Of The Mind

It was at this lowest ebb that I remember first hearing about 'the secret'. I can't remember how I heard about it or what made me want to read it but I was fascinated, I read the book and understood absolutely nothing consciously but I believe to this very day that my subconscious had a different idea. I think on some level I understood that this could be the catalyst to changing my life.

At that point however I believed that all I had to do was repeat affirmations to myself and everything would suddenly change. I wrote down you are loveable, you are happy, you have an amazing boyfriend etc and slept with these little notes under my pillow each and every night thinking that would do the trick, I have told the 'universe' what I want and now I just had to sit back and wait for it to happen.

That of course is not how it works – I may have had those little notes under my pillow but nothing else had changed, I wasn't doing the work, I didn't say them out loud, I didn't actually believe them, I was still telling myself at every opportunity that I was stupid and that I was alone and that I hated myself and that no-one loved me or would ever love me …….and so that is what life continued to give me.

Looking back however at my life after that point and knowing what I know now I did attract many things in to my life, good and bad using my mind and the power it has to either support us or completely derail us. I eventually met my now husband Steve because I had fallen heavily for another boy that I was at that time hanging out with.

I had two lifelong friends in my life, we had met when my mum was out painting the front gate at our house and they moved in three doors up. Sue was 4, I was 3 and Andy was 2. Even when mum died and I moved away to live in my step mums house we kept in touch and years later when Sue moved to New Zealand to live Andy and I hung out together a lot.

His best friend Paul was my first real crush (not including the many famous ones that I dreamt would sweep me off my feet and take me away from it all). I used to go over to Andy's house every weekend and we would drink heavily, he would smoke pot and Paul and I would roll our eyes and confide in each other that we didn't like it. He was the first boy I could actually really talk to (not including Andy of course) and I fell hard.

One day I mustered up all of my courage to tell him how I felt (bearing in mind all I have told you up to this point you can imagine how hard this was for me to do). It didn't go so well and I ended up being rejected, heartbroken and totally and utterly disgusted with myself for thinking anybody could feel that way about me. I decided there and then that I didn't care about having a relationship anymore, I could not bear the hurt from this new feeling on top of everything else that I felt about myself and so I told myself that I was destined to be alone anyway so why not just make peace with it.

Unknown to me back then this was my surrender, this was the point I didn't care, this was my letting go of the outcome. It wasn't that I didn't want to be loved or that I wanted to be alone forever BUT I gave up obsessively thinking about it at every waking minute of every single day and just stopped caring.

I still dreamt about being happy and getting married and having someone to love me nearly every night, but the difference – in my dreams and in my imagination I was thin, happy, completely and utterly loveable and completely and utterly adored by my partner. Put these two things together and you have a recipe for attraction. In the process of letting go and not actually caring anymore in my conscious mind I released all emotional attachment and all negativity to the process of finding someone. Dreaming about it and believing it in my subconscious mind told the universe to do its thing and the very next week I met my now husband.

Chapter 4 – That Was Only The Beginning

Now at this point you may be thinking that I had it made, I knew how to manifest, I had watched the secret, I had learnt about the power of letting go and not having an emotional attachment to anything – so now we live happily ever after right?

Not so fast.

I literally had no clue how I had attracted Steve into my life, I had no clue how to be a girlfriend, I had no clue how to love and allow myself to be loved in return and so the next chapter, however amazing it seemed like it was going to be, was probably harder than any other chapter in my life that came before it.

I actually had to let love in, I had to love someone, and I had to allow myself to be loved.

When mum died I had formed a belief that people who I love leave me. Mum had after all and after that so did my sister and to a certain extent my dad too.

Cathy was my big sister, the only one who knew what it was like and how I was feeling in the days, weeks, months and years following mum's death. We surely had to stick together, surely........

But she was struggling too, in some ways even more than I was, because she was three years older and had more emotional maturity than I did, she was also in the impressionable age range of being a tween, trying to cope with puberty, a dad who worked long hours and was never there, a little sister who probably increasingly annoyingly hung on her every word and all this with no mum to guide her.

She craved love to, and so she went out to find it herself, not content to let it find her, and so she left.

I remember I was staying at my nan's house the night I got a phone call from my dad to tell me Cathy was going to live somewhere else, that she wouldn't be there when I got back home. I didn't quite understand what that meant at the time but in the long run it meant that I lost my big sister. In her need to heal and to get off the emotional roller coaster, to make a better life for herself - even though if you asked her she'd fully admit she took the long route to do that, a route which caused considerable angst back then – she left me too.

She didn't mean to, but the only way to save herself was to leave me behind.

So out of the three people in my life who were my constants - mum died and left me, dad checked out and left me and Cathy had to run away to heal, and left me.

So my belief that people who I love leave made me harden my heart, made me so frightened to give all of myself away to anyone, made me scared to death of being in a relationship, that actually having the one thing I longed for, the relationship, was the thing that I found the hardest in all of my life and the thing that almost broke me.

I became a doormat in the worst sense of the word. I did everything in my power to be the perfect girlfriend, to never rock the boat, to never have an opinion, to never offer a suggestion, to never speak my truth, to never say what I really wanted to say – to never give Steve an excuse or a reason to leave.

I was shy, I was introverted, I was desperately critical of myself and the way I looked and acted, I was socially inept, I hated going out, hated socialising with anyone, making small talk or meeting new people and so I found being a girlfriend incredibly difficult.

SURVIVING TO THRIVING - A PRACTICAL GUIDE TO HELP YOU GO FROM BARELY LIVING TO LIVING WITH JOY

Everything about it was everything I dreaded.

My one saving grace throughout all of this was my love of football, my love of Liverpool, the place I now lovingly call my spiritual home, Anfield.

Steve was also a football fan, was also a Liverpool fan, and so we bonded over that joint passion and when attending football games together I could be completely myself, completely at ease, completely free from all of the noise in my head and the pain in my body – that girl was the one I think he fell in love with back then, that girl is the one that I aim to be in every single moment today.

And so somehow, despite all the odds we made it work, amazingly we are still together - only in this day and age as I write this book we have much more of an equal footing in the relationship, I am no longer a doormat for him or anyone......but more on that later.

Looking back, I caused most of the issues in our relationship both early on and in later years. I was damaged, I was hurting, I was in a very low place back then but unable to see it, unable to notice the signs and therefore unable to do anything to help myself or help Steve navigate his life with me. I was living in my own personal hell with no-one having any clue of how bad it was getting and me taking no responsibility for any of it, as far as I was concerned I was a victim of my life, everything was happening to me not as a result of me.

I now know that this was me taking absolutely no self-responsibility, I was living with a victim mentality and the longer I stayed there the harder it was for me to claw my way back. Yes, I had been riding an emotional roller coaster since mum died and I think anyone would have had scars, but I was unable to see that it was my choice to carry on riding it, it was my choice to not stop the ride and get off, it was my choice to carry on living the way I was.

Chapter 5 - Our Move And The Wedding

Oh if only I'd had the beauty of hindsight, how different my choices might have been.

You see I had a notion that if I could get away from the UK, if I could get away from my life as I knew it, if I could start again somewhere else, be in a place where no-one knew fat Jane, no-one knew unhealthy Jane, no-one knew damaged Jane, no-one knew self-conscious Jane then all of my issues would be solved, just like that.

In my head all I had to do was leave my old life, get on a plane and start a new one somewhere different and it would all be fine.

I literally decided to run away from my life.

The only problem with that was, it changed nothing, other than to pile on more and more despair.

I had now added guilt to the mix of things to hate myself for - guilt for leaving my dad, guilt for leaving Cathy before I had had a chance to heal the rift that was developing between us with every day that we didn't speak (to this day she has never met Steve and I have been with him 24 years as I write this paragraph) guilt for leaving my step sister who had just had a beautiful baby and therefore guilt for leaving my niece, my nephews, guilt for leaving my friends, my job – literally everything.

I remember the day before Steve was due to get on the plane to fly to New Zealand, he had found a job and was leaving before me, I was staying behind to sell our house and pack up our life and joining him when all that was done. We were sat in our front room due to say goodbye to one of his good friends and I wobbled massively. I burst into tears, I told him not to go, that I didn't want to, that it was the wrong decision

– he calmed me and told me that it was okay, if I really didn't want to do it then he would stay and we would carry on our life in the UK.

If only I had listened to my intuition and followed that fear, the part of me that knew somewhere deep down that I should not go, the part that today I would know to trust implicitly.

Instead I let him go and that decision would haunt me for many years that followed.

New Zealand seemed like an easy place to choose, we had friends there, we spoke the same language, everyone said it was very English and we would fit right in, we had got engaged on a visit to Christchurch a couple of years prior, it seemed perfect.

And for Steve it is, for me it will never be.

But I let him go, sold our house, packed up the rest of our life, got on a plane and left everything that I knew behind.

Running away from it all.

Running towards more of the same - same life, same feelings, same emotions, same self-hatred, just a different location.

I think this was the catalyst for me to become even sicker - my eating habits were now totally mine to dictate, I had no family anymore looking over my shoulder, telling me I wasn't eating enough, telling me I was doing too much exercise, telling me my skin looked drawn and puffy.

I was free to control the only thing in my life that I felt I had some control over – the amount I ate and the amount of exercise I did.

And please don't get the wrong idea here, don't blame Steve for not noticing the signs, for not caring as my family had. I was so good at hiding it all from him and from anyone else, no one else here in my new home knew my history and I was not going to tell them or show them any of it.

And so I spiralled, eating less, exercising more, losing no weight so hating myself more for being useless not even able to get a diet right. But once again I had pushed my body so much that it was hanging on to every single thing I ate to try and stay healthy.

"You can't even lose a bit of weight, what on earth is wrong with you, how utterly useless are you, you do know he is only staying with you until someone better, thinner, prettier comes along, he won't marry you, why on earth would he want to, you are so ugly he can do much better, you are fat and ugly with absolutely no personality, you may as well just end it now, your pathetic".

That was the constant barrage of abuse that I hurled at myself on a daily basis, it was never ending, I never gave myself a break, it was pure unadulterated hatred.

I found my wedding journal the other day, reading back through some of the things I wrote back then was heart-breaking.

One passage read "I hope Steve is okay and not dreading marrying me too much, I just want him to be happy" another read "I hope he actually turns up, I wonder why he actually wants to marry me, he could do so much better and I know he knows it" or "I had to go to the wedding venue first, normally it's the other way around and the groom has to go first, but only on my day would I have to stand there knowing he is not going to turn up and have to explain it to everyone, tell them that he deserves better than me, that he did the right thing not coming"

Literally heart-breaking. I had so much hate for myself I actually wonder now how I got through those years without actually going through with the thoughts that I had pretty much daily about ending it all and giving everyone a break.

But miraculously, as you may already know we did in fact get married, he did turn up, my thoughts and spiralling self hate didn't derail the day.

The only person they derailed was me, the only person they hurt was me, the only person they affected was me.

You see this is the problem with self hate, I had become so good at hiding it, so good at living day to day that no-one else noticed or knew about the narrative going on inside my head, playing on a loop over and over and over.

No-one had a clue.

I was the award winning actress in my own story, playing out the dutiful doormat of a girlfriend, never showing or saying what I really wanted to say, giving way too much of myself away, staying small, staying loveable, wanting to explode and say everything that was on my mind but fearing the absolute worst if I did.

I was the friend who was always there for others but never said what was on my mind, the sister who stayed meek and mild and wanted to please everyone while silently wanting to be able to say what I was really like, the workmate who never said no, always took on more and more and more because saying no could lead to disappointment and I could not bear to disappoint anyone.

I hid all of myself away, all of the time.

I was playing a role on the outside and silently screaming and dying on the inside.

Chapter Six - My Girls

My girls saved my life. I truly believe that they were sent to save me.

I had wanted to be a mum for my entire life. I knew that having children of my own meant that I would finally have the love I craved and be able to give love freely in return.

I struggled with love for the longest time, it's like a weird double edged sword, I crave it with all of my being and yet I am scared to give it because people I love leave, that was (and probably still is) my greatest fear in life.

But children are different, I would grow them, I would nurture them inside the womb and out, I would love them through every stage of their life, they would be mine so love was unconditional.

When I was told in no uncertain terms at the age of 22, literally 2 weeks into my relationship with Steve, that I would not be able to have children my world broke just a little bit more.

The one thing I had never questioned (weirdly because I had questioned being a partner, being a girlfriend, being a wife), the one thing that was holding me together I was now being told I wouldn't be able to have, the one thing I hadn't even considered not being a part of my life, I was being told wasn't going to be.......ever.

Cathy, my sister, had got pregnant at a young age because she craved love too and when she ran away to start her new life she did it by having a child, someone to love, someone to love her, someone to need her, someone she could give her everything too.

That's what I wanted, but instead I had PCOS, I had endometriosis, I had ovaries riddled with cysts and in a cruel twist of fate was put on birth control pills, not to stop any unwanted pregnancy but to control all of the other symptoms I was having.

The weight, the hairy face, the pimples, the bloating, the pain – things to make me hate myself even more.

I closed myself off just a little bit more that day.

I hardened my emotions and my heart to one more thing.

Bit by bit I was building a wall so high around my emotions and my ability to give and receive love that it would take a miracle to break down.

I was taking away my ability to love, and instead creating an internal monster of hate.

Looking back at it now and how it all played out once again I used the law of attraction, I used the law of vibration and the power of the mind – only I didn't know it.

The trouble is I used those laws in both good and bad ways. For many, many years I believed that doctor, I believed that what he told me was the truth and that there was absolutely no way I could ever have children. I got on with my life with my heart sad with longing for my baby, with hurt for something I had lost before I had even had it. And in that state, from that place, in that energy and with those thoughts and feelings I was telling my mind and body that I was never going to have any children, that the thing I longed for wasn't to be, that it was useless, that I was not destined to be a mum, again something I had failed at, what a pathetic excuse for a woman I was, I couldn't even do the one thing women are designed to do, reproduce.

I remember watching women around me at work and in the town where I lived, at shopping malls, on the beach, even my own family back in the UK having babies, being pregnant, happy and carefree with their big bellies and expectant faces. I would see pregnant women everywhere; it was like they were haunting me.

I was putting out into the universe that I was desperate for a baby, always thinking about being pregnant and having babies but at the same time having all these negative, critical feelings that it was never going to happen for me.

Talk about mixed signals.

Looking back at it now knowing all about the reticular activating system I was literally programming myself to see pregnant women everywhere, to notice every single one of them - all I was doing was saying to the universe I want to see babies and pregnant women everywhere please to remind me that I can't have this for myself.

It was debilitating and exhausting, and so very, very sad.

I knew that if I carried on the way I was that I would hurt myself in some way, I was becoming desperate, feeling slightly unhinged and that scared me enough to ask for help. It scared me into praying – something I had never done, something that was totally alien to me, something that surprised me.

But I remember sitting at the side of my bed and asking the universe for help. Over and over again, crying and desperate, hurting and feeling so very powerless I surrendered it all over to someone else because it was too much for me to bear anymore, I was at breaking point and I knew it.

I don't quite remember how long it took but somewhere in the next few days the name of a doctor crossed my path, Dr Anna Fenton. I had no idea who she was, what she did or how she could help me but I knew as soon as I heard her name that I had to look her up, a voice in my head was saying, trust me, this is your chance, take it.

So I made an appointment, I went to see her, we made a plan, executed that plan and the rest as they say is history. My baby girl, Chloe was born just over a year later, three months taking medication to induce a period, being prodded and poked, being stripped of all my dignity and then nine months spent pregnant.

I believe now looking back that my sitting in pain in my bedroom asking the universe to help me was the point it changed, the point where I gave control over to something greater than me, was the dark day of the soul that people talk about where it becomes just so much to handle that its either do or die. The Point the universe (or god, whatever you want to call it) takes over and delivers what you want. The point I had come across many times in my life up to that day and beyond without knowing it, without any knowledge of what I was doing.

Chapter 7 - A Stay at Home Mum and the Quake that Rocked my World……Literally

It's interesting isn't it, how life plays with you – here I was married to my one and only boyfriend, a new mum, with a beautiful baby girl, the two things I craved, love and motherhood but yet I was faced with another hurdle to drag myself over, I had to decide what I would do about my career.

The thought of going back to work and leaving Chloe with someone else, letting someone else essentially bring her up was heart-breaking. I had longed for this, I had wanted this, I was made for this.

So I decided to become a stay at home mum which actually just added to my issues with self-esteem and lack of self-worth – I was successful in my role as a careers adviser, I was professional and I was extremely good at my job, I hadn't actually realised it but this was holding me together in the dark days, my job was making me feel worthy, making me feel I was actually capable of doing something well, and so when I took this away from myself my mind went in to over-drive.

I became more and more introverted, I was cut off from the world by staying at home. As much as I loved being home, being with Chloe and taking care of her the decision to be at home and to essentially isolate myself was probably not a good thing for me.

The years that followed were filled with so many ups and downs, such highs and lows all intertwined together, it was mind spinning how I could be so happy with Chloe one minute and so low and depressed and scared and homesick the next.

I was on a perpetual roller coaster and it was scary.

Steve and I made the decision in that time to try for another baby. This time I wouldn't have any fertility treatment, I was I believe looking back, starting to trust my intuition just ever so slightly and so if I was meant to have another baby then it would happen naturally.

Hannah was born nine months later.

This pregnancy was harder, I was constantly sick, tired with a toddler to look after, depressed, not caring about myself or my appearance. I was lonely, I felt like I had no purpose in the world (other than being Chloe's mum) and my confidence, which was obviously never great to start with, fell to an all-time low even for me.

And, on the 4th September 2010 a week prior to my finding out I was pregnant, Christchurch suffered a 7.1 magnitude earthquake.

Funnily enough I was okay with that, yes it had been scary in the moment that it was happening but I was from the UK, I had no idea what being in an earthquake actually meant. I stupidly thought I had survived it, everyone I knew was okay, it was over now and life could move on.

Oh how wrong I was.

Being pregnant in a time when constant aftershocks are literally rocking your world was awful. I needed to have a 12 week scan but because Christchurch was suffering aftershocks from the quake all the time, sometimes many times in a day, services were not running to time or to plan so when my 12-week scan showed all the markers for Downs Syndrome (a thick nuchal translucency and raised hCG levels alongside my being 37 years old at the time) I needed to have an amniocentesis.

The problem was that I couldn't have this scan for many weeks and so by the time I would find out if my baby had downs or not I would be well into my pregnancy, over 20 weeks into it. I had to spend 8 weeks in a constant state of fear from the aftershocks and fear that my baby may not be well which made bonding during pregnancy really hard for me. I wasn't sure how to feel, I didn't know how to react to this, I was finding life really tough, again.

The procedure itself was actually okay truth be told, yes it was scary having a big needle inserted into my tummy, but it showed that my beautiful Hannah was fine, perfectly normal and so I told myself that I could now relax and enjoy being pregnant, as I had with Chloe.

Then came the devastating earthquake, the aftershock of the first event that, although not as strong in magnitude, was horrific.

I will never forget the 22nd February 2011. It was just before 1pm (12.51pm to be exact), I had just put Chloe down for her afternoon nap in her room and was making myself a cup of tea when it struck.

I never thought I would live through something like that, something so terrifying.

In my hurry to get back to Chloe from the kitchen I fell over in the hallway, the quake was so strong it literally threw me to the ground, right on my belly, right on my unborn baby with such a force it took the wind out if me.

The next part of that day happened in a daze, I got Chloe up, I went outside on the deck of my house, feeling safer out of the building than in it, a neighbour brought me over a wind up radio so I could hear the news coverage. All power, all systems like internet, phone, sewage, water had gone.

I was bleeding a lot and my tummy was cramping.

But I couldn't deal with that just yet I was hearing reports of buildings having fallen down in the city centre where Steve was, people trapped, people killed. I tried to ring him but nothing was working, I couldn't get through, I had no idea if he was okay.

It took 6 hours before I knew that he was safe.

When I saw him walk up the driveway having walked most of the way home, I have never been so relieved in all my life. And just like that the bleeding and the cramping that I had been ignoring since my fall, stopped.

I had to wait almost another week before I could be checked over by my midwife but finally she told me that Hannah was okay, my baby was safe, she was a little fighter and had come through unscathed.

Unlike me.

I not only felt alone, homesick and scared, I also now felt unsafe in my own home, in the country that we had decided to live in and totally responsible for keeping my girls safe in a state of constant strong aftershocks, no services that we all take for granted, cooking on a BBQ and bathing in a bucket in the garage, with a portaloo at the end of the road that we lived on – that was my life for a good few weeks after the quake.

Somewhere in that state my step mum died of the very same cancer that had taken my mum all those years before, my dad was left alone again and I had so much guilt around living in New Zealand and not being in England with him, to take care of him, leaving that job up to my step sisters and step brother – they were doing a job that I should have been doing. Just one more thing to add to the list of things that made me selfish, worthless, never good enough, and now a terrible daughter.

I know that at this point you are all thinking why didn't I just leave, with all that going on why didn't we just go home. It's a question I ask myself daily, I know the answer – Steve didn't want to - he was happy (and still is) in New Zealand and he could not see himself moving back to the UK, it was just not something he wanted to do and I was not strong enough to push, was not confident enough in myself or the love he felt for me to push, I felt that if I rocked the boat and made my feelings clear he would leave me, he would stay in New Zealand and I would go home alone with my two girls and deprive them of having a dad, something I just couldn't do, no matter how bad I felt, my feelings didn't matter, I wasn't worthy of having what I wanted, I just had to get on with it, I wasn't good enough, loveable enough, any type of enough to keep him if I pushed - that's what I told myself, that's why I stayed.

Chapter 8 – Network Marketing

What I did next might have seemed like a very strange decision, I joined a network marketing company selling make up.

I was not interested in make up, I hardly ever wore it, I had no clue how to put it on, I never ever took a selfie, I had no friends who were into make up to sell it to and to be honest I was completely at a loss as to where to start.

But something in my body, in my being, in my intuition told me to take the leap, to do it anyway despite all my fears.

For once I decided to listen.

The thing that drew me in was that it was an online based business which meant that I could hide behind my computer and pretend. The introverted, confidence lacking, tired, depressed side of me loved that – and social media was something that I was good at. I used Facebook daily, it was my lifeline to the UK, to my family and my friends back home – it meant I could potentially earn a bit of money to make me feel I was contributing something to our family life. I was on social media anyway so why not try.

But I sucked big time.

I hated selling, I hated trying to make that make up look good while all around me other presenters (that's what we called ourselves) had amazing make up skills, were young and glamorous and talented, everything I wasn't.

I felt like mutton dressed as lamb, like a sleazy salesperson, I was pushing myself to do selfies and lives - feeling like an imposter, it was awful. The feeling that I needed to push and hustle for ever sale, for every promotion, I was showing up online in ways that felt alien to me, totally inauthentic, fake and in truth buying more and more of the products myself to make the targets, to make the sales, to make the promotions, to get the accolades. All the time knowing that I didn't deserve them, that I knew were fake and false and just made me feel like a total fraud.

I stuck it out for a long time because as bad as the sales and targets side of it felt, it was leading me down a different path, it was introducing me once more to self-development. All those thoughts from years ago when I read 'the secret' were suddenly being sparked in my brain again only this time I was an adult, I was older, I was more mature and I understood it all so much better.

Those years in network marketing allowed me to grow as a person and forever changed me, something I will always be grateful for. The more books I read, the more people I learnt about and the more I delved into the self-development side of network marketing the more I silenced that bully in my head, the more I changed the thoughts I had about myself and the more I started to like things about myself.

Don't get me wrong, it took so much time for things to change, so much effort to do the things in the books and the things I was learning – this work when the total opposite is so ingrained in your head, and has been for so long is effort, its gruelling sometimes, it takes you into the dark places, it has to, to then be able to lead you back out into the light.

But little by little I noticed that when you start to work on your mind everything changes, I began to see that even though there was so many things I had been through and so many things in my life I didn't like, that by not focussing on them, not focussing on the negatives and seeing the positives for probably the first time ever I began to grow as a person, I began to trust my own intuition and trust in myself, which was huge for me.

I started to feel grateful for my life, who who knew this was possible.

I found a passion for something again, other than motherhood.

I started to really delve in to the law of attraction, in to mind-set and more specifically the reticular activating system, I studied as a life coach, a law of attraction practitioner, a manifestation/mindfulness specialist and added many modalities such as numerology, EFT and meditation to my skillset. I am not saying that you have to do any of this (reading this book is totally enough) but truth be told I wanted to, I was like a sponge, soaking it all up, I literally couldn't get enough.

I knew I was good at coaching from my life before motherhood and I had a passion for self-development. I began to immerse myself into it in a massive way. Learning all I could about the mind and body connection and how my thoughts could either save me or bury me, something I was all too familiar with.

And then my soul kicked in big time and a spark was lit, I fed that spark with more and more and more and suddenly the fire was raging. I was learning that I could love my body, be confident in my own skin and know my own mind.

Being led by my soul, leaning in to my intuition and feeling brave and powerful for probably the first time in my entire life felt amazing to me, and I wanted more and more of that feeling, I didn't want the old Jane to come back, ever again.

Now I am making it my life's mission to show everybody that life can be wondrous and all the things we dream about can be ours if we only learn the keys to unlocking them.

Abundance in all areas of our life, not just monetary, is our birth-right, there is absolutely enough for all of us and so we don't need to be negative and jealous of anyone or anything, we don't need to feel stuck in any area of our life.

There is so much stress and negativity in the world, everywhere we go we are bombarded with it and as women especially I think we feel we have to look a certain way and act a certain way and dress a certain way to be valued, I don't conform to that anymore, that world view was at the root of my eating disorder for many years, I was striving to be that perfect woman with the perfect body and the perfect face, and I could never live up to it because its fake and I am not perfect, no-one is.

So at the root of everything for me is authenticity, when we are confident enough to show all sides of ourselves, when we truly show up as ourselves and start to care less about what people think of us and to conform to the box life wants to put us in, that's when real change happens.

I want to make an impact by showing people the power of mind-set and the power that we all have within ourselves. I honestly believe if we all started to live more from our intuition, from our own internal GPS, from our truth, then the world would be a much kinder, wiser and more compassionate place to be and that is the legacy I want to leave people with.

Through what I have learnt on my path I now teach my clients to connect with their intuition more and to trust themselves. Our body knows what's right and what's wrong, we have just forgotten to ask it, we always have the answers within ourselves if only we would trust that we do.

I think women, and mums especially, put so many people's needs before their own, there is a reason why we are told to put on our own lifejackets first. We need to learn self love, we need to learn to value ourselves more, to see our own importance.

More often than not that's the place I start with my clients now, building their own self love muscle, the rest flows so easily after that. But it has to start, and it has to start now wherever you are right in this moment.

So, in the following chapters of this book I want to give you the things that have made the biggest difference for me, the elements of what I do that have had the biggest impact on my life. I want everyone to know and to understand that life is there waiting for us, that we can truly change our self-perception, our world perception, we just have to learn how to unlock the keys to our mind and our body and our intuition and I want to hand my keys over to you, it's up to you to take them.

It's up to you to put into practice what I am about to teach you, I can give you everything I know that has made massive changes in my life. You can read it all here in the following pages and I hope you enjoy and feel inspired by every single word but I need to be clear about something right here, right now……..reading this is not enough.

Reading it and half-heartedly using it will be like I was back in the day when I put those notes under my pillow and thought everything was going to change. The truth is it won't, this will only work if you commit to it, if you make a promise with yourself to do the tasks, to be honest with yourself, to dig deep and to really commit to change, if you are willing to do that this could be the most important book you ever read.

Chapter Nine – Feeling into Fear

I started a long time ago to not make new year's resolutions anymore and instead began to start a practice of having a word of the year. As I write this book we are living in the aftermath of 2020 with the pandemic and what we all lived through and I made my word for 2021 'Fearless'.

It was a word that resonated with me on so many levels. I didn't talk to many people about the virus and what was happening in the world, not because I didn't care or because I wasn't aware, not because I wasn't sympathetic to what was going on, not because I live in New Zealand and its okay for me, not because I didn't understand it and certainly not because it didn't affect me - the truth is it did affect me, in July of 2020 my nieces were due to fly to New Zealand to come and visit me, then I was flying back with them for a family holiday and a month long trip in the UK. After all I have said about being homesick and loving my time with family you can understand how devastated I was that it all had to be cancelled.

At that time, I didn't know when I would ever get home again, when I would get to see my family again, when I would step off that plane in Manchester and feel enveloped with love, when I would feel relief to be home.

And so my decision not to talk about it wasn't because it didn't affect my life. I didn't talk about it because I understand now that how much fear or negativity I have in my life affects my energy. To me in my life today everything is energy and energy affects everything.

Focusing on the fear, pandering to what the media wanted us to see and feel, none of that helped anyone, none of that made any difference to what might or might not happen, none of that changed what the virus did or didn't do.

If I was drawn into it all and started to feel feelings of sadness, fear, anger, frustration - the virus was still around or on the flip side if I stayed in my own lane and experienced feelings of happiness, calmness, joy and gratitude - the virus was still around.

So I chose the latter, because thoughts, feelings and emotions become things and so I will not choose negativity ever anymore, now I choose optimism, happiness, peace and calmness. I chose to keep my energy high and not worry about things I can't control.

I have learnt that becoming free from fear in my life is not about becoming ego driven or selfish its actually about fearing less, not caring less. So I decided with all that was going on around me to make that my word of the year for 2021 – I was going to fear-less.

I used to practice new year's resolutions all the time. I used to get to the 31st of December and I'd be thinking right what's my new year's resolution going to be, what am I going to do this year that's different, what am I going to do that I'm going to hold myself accountable to and keep. And I would think of all these really hard things and then put massive pressure on myself to keep that promise I made, to keep my resolution.

And yet by the third week or the fourth week of January each and every year I'd broken it, the diet, that thing I said I wouldn't do, the exercise plan, etc, etc and then I'd just feel bad.

That pressure feeds into the feeling that I'd let myself down and then fear pops up and failure and all kinds of not enough-ness. Once I recognised this in myself I knew I didn't want to feel that way anymore and I don't want you to have those feelings either. So from now on don't make new year's resolutions, have a word of the year instead. If you are reading this in January, brilliant, if not why does it have to be January anyway, who says we have to make that the new start? You could even expand on this even further and have a different word every month based on your dreams and your wants for any given period of your life. Just pick something that fits what you want to do or become moving forward.

For me it could have been alignment, it could have been joy, it could have been happy, it could have been flexibility, there are so many words that you could choose. Feel in to it and see what resonates.

The one thing to understand with this and to understand about why I chose fearless didn't mean that I wasn't ever going to feel fear ever again, because truth be told I do, every single day at some moment I feel fear but the difference now is that I'm not going let it impact my life the way it used to, I am not going to let it control me, I am not going to let that voice in my head be the one that takes over and runs my day. That is what being fear less and fearing less is all about, and the more you do it the better at it you become and the more it becomes second nature.

The definition of fear if you look it up in the dictionary is "an unpleasant emotion caused by the threat of danger pain or harm".

We all have something in our brain called the reticular activating system and its primary purpose is to stop us from getting into any harmful situations, to stop us feeling danger, to keep us alive basically.

Back in the stone age when we lived in those times and there were bears and tigers and lions and we were living in our caves and we were primitive that was really useful, nowadays not so much and yet we're still living with this part of our brain, the reticular activating system, giving us the same messages, telling us I've got to keep you safe, I've got to keep you safe, there's harm, there's harm, there's harm and that's what it floods our brains with and that's why we feel fear.

However, the good news is that it's actually quite easy to rewire the belief systems that we have and to change what our reticular activating system actually looks for in our day to day lives.

The biggest times that I feel fear is when I don't trust myself, when I don't trust that things are going to work out for me, when I don't trust that I'm on the right path and when I don't trust that the messages I'm being given are the right ones. Being able to tune into your intuition and actually listen to what its telling you is paramount. Knowing that we are always being guided and always being protected, that we all have the answers within ourselves, it's just being in tune enough with the part of ourselves that is our higher selves and being able to trust that what we are being asked to do, the path we are being asked to follow is the right one and trusting implicitly that where we are being led is perfect for us.

Once you are able to really get into that space and live your life from a place of knowing, from not caring what other people may say, what judgements they may pass, what opinions they may have, that's true freedom. Being able to stop the outside influences from overpowering the internal voice.

I want you to just think for a moment how your life would be different if you actually didn't care what other people thought about you, what would you do differently, how would you act differently, what things would you be doing, what would you allow yourself to portray, what would you be putting out to the world?

It's a big loaded question but as we move through this book together I really want you to think about that because it's the key to it all.

When I was younger I heard my dad say 'children should be seen and not heard' a lot and that is one statement I swore I would never say to my own children. For so many years I was meek and mild and I believed that I shouldn't be heard and that I didn't have a voice, that I didn't have anything good or useful to say to anybody. From a very early age I'd been programmed to believe from that statement that I should be seen but not heard.

Don't be too excitable, don't be overly confident, don't be too loud, don't be silly, don't live in dream world, you can't possibly do that - how many of you heard those types of statements, those types of comments growing up?

Those seemingly insignificant throw away comments flood our brains as children with reasons to feel fear, with reasons to play small, with reasons to not be seen, to stay in the shadows, to drown our voices to not listen to the internal part of ourselves that says differently.

If you learned to shut those influences out, if you learned to change them into empowering statements how different could your life be?

So starting right now you're going to take back your power. From this point forward whenever you hear one of those statements, one of those comments replaying in your mind that have been keeping you stuck you are going to tell yourself not to listen, you are going to tell yourself you've got this, you've got this, you've got this, you're not scared anymore, you're in control now.

Using powerful affirmations can be a catalyst for changing the reticular activating system. Saying empowering statements to yourself every day instead of negative statements.

Close your eyes right now and repeat this affirmation:

"Fear, thank you for showing me what I am scared of, thank you for guiding me, thank you for showing me where I need to be stronger, I am ready now to embrace my fears because they have helped me to grow. Facing my fear is empowering but I give myself permissions to let it go now, to be brave, to be fearless"

Repeat that to yourself, thank your past fears for showing you that you have grown, that there are things you no longer need to be scared of, for showing you that you love and respect yourself enough to stop listening to the voice inside your head, to have evolved enough to not be held back, for showing you and your reticular activating system that you are not in any danger.

If you keep on affirming this truth and stopping the fearful thoughts before they infiltrate your brain that helps you surrender, it helps you begin to trust your intuition, it helps you to begin to regain your control, it helps you to begin to believe in yourself and to believe that there really is nothing to be scared of.

Take Away Task:

I want you to create a voice recording, it can be on your phone, it can be on your iPad, it can be on your computer, it can be absolutely anywhere but I want you to create a voice recording of your own voice for 20 seconds just saying these words:

"I trust myself completely, I no longer listen to my fears, I am in control, I have the ability in any moment to choose again and I choose love. I trust myself completely, I no longer listen to my fears, I am in control, I have the ability in any moment to choose again and I choose love. I trust myself completely, I no longer listen to my fears, I am in control, I have the ability in any moment to choose again and I choose love"

Record your voice and play that recording back to yourself at least five times during the day. It is imperative that it is your voice because the most powerful voice that you can listen to is your own, when you hear yourself saying the words your brain assimilates them so much quicker than anyone else saying them to you, it then believes them quicker than if anyone else said them to you. This simple task alone is powerful.

Chapter Ten – Where Did It Come From?

In the previous chapter we talked about where your fears come from and how to stop them. In this chapter I want to explore that a little bit more.

I want you to think about where in your life you feel scared, where you have doubt, where you feel overwhelm – these are the areas that give you the most fear. Whether you see it as a fear or not, it is. It's the thing you don't want to face, it's the thing that you know you have to change but you have no idea where to start.

For me one of the biggest things when I was in the middle of my own journey was speaking up, communicating how I really felt, the fear of being seen. I had been told over and over to be seen and not heard and so that manifested itself into a fear of putting myself out there, of being noticeable, of being judged, a fear of what will people think of me, a fear of being too old, to fat, too whatever........

Whatever you think about when I ask you to think of your biggest area of concern I am absolutely sure is something that you have held on to for a long time. It will stem from something, somewhere, or from someone.

However, how many of you can pinpoint the exact moment that that fear was given to you, the first time you felt it, the first time it caused you not to do something?

One of the ways I work with my clients is to use the analogy of an onion, to peel back all of the layers and open you up to the very core, the place where that feeling first originated.

I think about my fear of being judged, sharing my truth, being visible, that stemmed from within my childhood. I heard children should be seen and not heard so many times that my brain took it as truth and therefore I developed a fear of putting myself out there, of sharing my voice, of being who I was.

Think about it, think of your own, fears such as fear of flying, fear of driving, fear of spiders, fear of going outside, fear of lifts, fear of confined spaces etc - where do they come from? where do they actually stem from?

No one is born with a fear of spiders, or a fear of flying. As a baby you don't even know what a spider is, you have not even been on a plane so how do you have a fear of flying when you don't even know what it feels like?

Someone has given that fear to you, someone has made you feel the fear, it's a learned behaviour.

When you can recognise that and peel back the layers of the onion, of the fear, and uncover the middle, the core, the root, that tells us where it came from.

So I want you to write down your biggest fears, I want you to come up with whatever it is that stops you from living your life freely, from being you, from doing things that you want to do. Whatever you can think of I want you to write it down and really dig down deep. Think about what it is that impacts your life, what fears you have that stop you living your truth.

Now go back into your subconscious mind and think about the stories that are lying there - what is the first time that you remember feeling this fear, what were you doing, where were you, who were you with? where did it actually stem from initially?

SURVIVING TO THRIVING - A PRACTICAL GUIDE TO HELP YOU GO FROM BARELY LIVING TO LIVING WITH JOY

I promise you the answers are all in there they're just locked down deep because this is a fear that you have carried sometimes for your entire life and we have already established that your reticular activating system wants to keep you safe, it doesn't want you to remember, it wants to stop you from doing things that it deems unsafe and allowing you to release this goes against what it sees to be its role in your life - keeping you safe, therefore keeping you stuck.

But if you do the work, if you peel the layers, if you dig deep, if you trust your intuition, if you trust the answers you are being given as you do this exercise you can and will access where it comes from, and once you access the stories that preclude the feeling, that's when you will see that it's not true, that's when you will begin to recognise that it's just a story and it stemmed from somewhere else, not from within you.

That's when you know that you don't have to listen to it anymore and that's when you free yourself.

So keep peeling back those layers, journal whatever comes to mind. There is no wrong or right way to do this, it doesn't have to make sense to your rational brain, just write, just write whatever comes into your mind and within that writing, within the subconscious brain, within what you're being given is what you need to hear.

A belief that you have held all your life is really powerful and when you hold tight onto a belief your subconscious you will do anything in your power to make that belief true, you will do anything in your power to keep looking for the signs that make it true, because the alternative is scary, the alterative can turn your world on its head. You want to believe that its real because it has held you back.

When you uncover or feel anything in your life the most powerful questions to ask is, is this true or is this something I have been given?

Once we can get to the point of asking is this true? And the answer is no we can begin to change the narrative.

There will always be something in your past, an experience, something that you did, something somebody said, that planted the seed, that made you think this thing, there will be something deep inside you that made you have this particular belief about yourself, about your life so make a pact with yourself right now to stop listening to those old stories, stop listening to the messages that were given to you, from other people, from childhood, from school, because they don't serve us anymore, they are not empowering us to move forward and to do better and they're simply not true.

Success is always at the end of failure so stop being scared of putting yourself out there, of doing the thing that you don't enjoy or that makes you feel the fear because it's only by failing and doing it again and doing it again and doing it again and doing it again that you will tell your subconscious brain actually this is okay, this is good, I'm not feeling as bad now, I'm actually okay doing this thing.

The more you do that, the more you override your subconscious, the more you change and show your reticular activating system that this is not something that that we need to be kept safe from anymore, it's actually okay. When you start to look for the belief that it's safe and not the belief that it's fearful you will actually change the neural pathways within your brain.

The loudest message is always the one that's heard so if you can begin to say to yourself when you get on that plane or you get in that car or you get in the lift or you press the go live button on Facebook it's okay, I am not scared, the truth is this is not my fear, this was given to me from somewhere else, I don't have to feel fearful of this anymore, that is when you begin to evolve and to dissipate it and never have to feel it again.

Instead of oh my god I don't like this, I'm feeling scared, what if this happens, what if that happens, what if I get stuck, what if we have a crash, what if I hit the accelerator instead of the brake, what if we get lots of turbulence on the plane - whatever it is if you stand at that beginning and actually do some deep breathing exercises, quieten your brain and give yourself a new message, a new normal, is this true? No? so therefore I'm not scared, I've got this, this is not my fear, this was given to me from somewhere else, this is not mine to keep, I release it.

I remember back in the day when I first started on my journey in network marketing I was petrified of doing videos, I was petrified of talking on social media, I was petrified of pressing the record button – my finger would sit and hover over that record or play button and the voices, the fears would start - oh my god what if I mess up, what if I can't remember what I'm going to say, what if nobody listens, what if nobody watches, what if I get some hate comments, what if people think that I'm too old for this, to ugly, mutton dressed as lamb, what if people think who on earth is she to be telling me this, to be teaching me this stuff, a constant barrage of fear and hate for myself and what I was about to do.

I would sit there and all of those thoughts would come into my head and stop me from doing what I was going to do, and I let it, I never once had the wherewithal to ask is this true?

Where did this come from? Who is this fear from, what does this tell me? Is this children should be seen and not heard replaying again and again and again?

Now I don't care, I don't actually care if people think what I'm saying is dribble because those people who think that are not my people, are not my audience, are not who I am trying to reach.

I have an absolutely deep seated belief in myself and what I'm saying and what I'm teaching and the messages that I am putting out into the world, I know with absolute certainty that this stuff works, that it is life changing because I have lived it and I am here doing it and I know that all of the things that I can give you and share with you make a difference, I am not the person I was two, three years ago - even one year ago – I am not the same person because I continue to grow, and I continue to up level and I continue to evolve and that is truly loving without fear.

Personal growth can do so much for you, it changes you inside which changes you outside. It's such an amazing thing and journaling is a big part of that because when you get down to the root of the problem and where it actually came from you change for good.

Take Away task:

Write down your fears, write down the old beliefs around those fears - why you think you have them and where did they come from.

It doesn't have to make sense, just get it out on paper, brain dump it all onto the page and then ask yourself is this belief real or is it a story that you've been holding on to? is it somebody else's fear, has it been given to you by somebody else? If so, who? where did it come from?

Once you have your fears on paper look at them, really look at them, pick the top two or three things that are really causing you pain and flip them. Write an affirmation which flips the belief and actually changes the neural pathway in the brain to make that the new stronger belief.

I am afraid of being seen, what if I look silly becomes I am brave and I know that what I'm saying needs to be heard.

Repeat this new affirmation to yourself over and over and over and over like a broken record until that belief becomes the loudest one that you hear, until that belief overpowers the old one that you no longer need to listen to, that no longer serves you in any way.

Chapter 11 - Taking Your Abundance Pulse

As painful as it can be the very first thing I like anyone I work with to do is start with where they are right now, look at every area of their life, evaluate it all and figure out which parts need work and which parts are actually serving them well already. I like to call this 'taking your abundance pulse".

By looking at life and expanding even further on where your beliefs come from we are able to really drill down into what we actually want for ourselves and this in turn enables us to set powerful intentions for change. What I have found from both my own life and others who I have helped is that it's really difficult to shift something in our reality if we are not absolutely clear on where we sit with it at this very minute.

So ask yourself the question – how abundant do you feel right now? Not just in monetary terms but in everything. Your health, your relationships, your career, your surroundings, your family, internally? Look at it all and ask yourself how it feels.

To help you with this you can use a powerful coaching tool called the wheel of life. Using this tool helps you to raise your awareness of what you have and what you may be missing and awareness of it is absolutely the key to changing it.

Start by getting a blank piece of paper and drawing a large circle in the middle of the page. Then divide your circle into eight sections. I like to start by dividing it in half, then quarters, then sixths then into eight equal shaped pieces of pie or pizza or whatever you may imagine your slices to be.

We are now going to give each slice a category or heading if you like.

Personal – meaning your self worth and how you see yourself?

Romance – how satisfied you are with your intimate relationships?

Family and friends – how do you see those other people on your life?

Career – Do you enjoy your job, are you fulfilled by it?

Money – Do you have enough, or are you lacking in this areas?

Health and Vitality – How do you feel in your mind and body?

Your Surroundings – Do you enjoy your home and where you live?

Fun and Life Experiences – What do you experience in any spare time you have; do you have fun?

Now I want you to assess each area of your pie or pizza and mark it on how well you feel it is going and how satisfied you are with it on a scale from 0 to 10 with 0 being absolutely awful and totally unsatisfied and 10 being incredible and extremely satisfied.

You could use the questions below to help you assess where you are and what score you want to give.

Personal

How worthy do you feel?

Do you feel you deserve all that you dream of?

How much self love do you have?

Do you treat yourself with kindness or are you very critical of yourself?

How much trust do you have in your decision making?

Are you connected to your inner being or your intuition?

Do you listen to yourself when you know you are given guidance?

Are you connected to spirit?

Are you aware of and connected to your emotions?

Do you allow yourself to be happy or do you feel stuck?

Romance

How do you feel about your current relationship status?

Do you feel supported?

Do you feel seen in your own right, are your views taken into consideration?

How much love and adoration do you feel?

Are you happy with your intimacy levels?

Are you able to express all that you want to?

Do you have good and open communication?

Family and Friends

How accepted do you feel by those in your life?

How close are your relationships?

Would you like more contact with friends or family?

Do you have the necessary support that you need?

Do you feel alone?

How are your views seen by others?

What do your family and friends mean to you?

Career

Do you enjoy your work?

Are you fulfilled and inspired by what you do?

How valued do you feel in your workplace?

Do you feel you are in the right career?

Would you like to further your qualifications or change completely?

Do you feel supported at work?

Do you earn what you feel you should?

Do you have good work and life balance?

Money

Are you satisfied with the money you have?

Do you feel lack or abundance in this area?

Are you living hand to mouth or is there always money left over?

How well do you manage your money?

Do you set financial goals?

Do you overspend or can you stick to a budget?

Do you always feel like you deserve or want more money?

Health and Vitality

Do you look after your body and your health?

How much energy do you feel?

Do you feel strong and vibrant?

Do you exercise regularly to get the endorphins flowing?

Do you have aches and pains?

Do you get enough sleep or are you burning the candle at both ends?

Do you feel and look your age, younger or older?

Surroundings

Do you like where you live?

How safe do you feel?

How satisfied are you with your home and possessions?

Do you feel inspired by your living arrangements?

Do your surroundings feel like home?

Are you constantly comparing your home to others?

Do you wish you lived somewhere else?

Fun and Life Experiences

Do you have fun?

Could you have more fun in your life?

Do you have enough down time to relax and rejuvenate?

Do you go on holiday?

As a family are you connected?

Do you experience pleasure daily?

Do you have hobbies you enjoy?

Do you have enough interests that you value?

Are you happy?

The trick with this exercise is to go with your gut feeling, whatever number comes up for you when you think of the area you are ranking, that is the correct score. Go with it and be okay with it whatever it is. There is no good or bad here, the answer you come up with allows you to pinpoint where change most needs to happen. Once you have the number for each area of your wheel of life draw a corresponding line on your piece of paper and then shade that part in. So for example if you felt your career was a 0 then you would leave the whole piece devoid of colour but if you felt your surroundings was a 5 then you would shade half of your piece for that corresponding section and maybe family and friends is a 10 then all of that piece would be shaded..

When I do this exercise, and I do it quite often so I can see my continual improvement or where things may have slid a little in my life, I colour my sections in different colours. That way, when everything is ranked and coloured it's easy to see how balanced or how full the good areas of your wheel of life is and equally easy to see where there is a little room, or a lot of room where improvements have to be made.

Doing this brings clarity to your life and shows you easily where there are areas you feel despondent about or on the flip side it shows areas of your life right now where you may be blissfully happy and content, that's good because it shows that there are parts to work on but it also shows there are parts to have gratitude for and to love.

Take Away Task:

Don't just read about this exercise, complete it and then ask yourself how it felt? Did the results hold any surprise for you, were there areas you thought you were good but actually need improvement?

Take your time to really feel into this and be okay with whatever your outcome is, grieve for the areas that are not balanced right now but also celebrate those that are.

Recognize that this is only the beginning, this is where you get to see where the most of the work needs to take place and that is a truly good thing. This exercise is transformative which is why it's a tool found abundantly in coaching and counselling all over the world.

Chapter Twelve – Step Into Your New Life

If you follow spiritual teachers such as Esther Hicks, Neville Goddard or more recently Gabby Bernstein you will already know that they all talk a great deal about visualization being the key to everything.

In many of her talks and books and podcast episodes Gabby Bernstein said that she would visualize herself as a best-selling author even before she had even started writing her first book. She knew that it was something she wanted to put out into the world because she had an overriding instinctive knowing that her journey could help a lot of people.

So in her mind she became the author, she put herself into her new life, the future life that hadn't happened yet, she stepped into that vision of herself even before she had any evidence that it would happen.

Visualisation is a powerful tool to use to flood your brain with images of things that you want to achieve, ways you want your life to change as opposed to thing you don't.

If you have a fear of flying chances are when you book a flight the days leading up to that flight are filled with worry, what if we get into bad weather, what if there is turbulence, what if I have to grip the side of the seats so tightly because I am scared the plane may not make it?

Instead try visualising the flight going well, you get the window seat that you love, the take-off and landing is the best you've ever experienced, you even manage to get a bit of sleep and before you know it the journey is over and you haven't felt scared at all.

You can choose which of those scenario's to play in your head leading up to that flight, you can choose, you always have a choice. If you get into the habit of visualising scenarios before they take place you can alter the way you experience those things.

There's actually a tool called segment intending which is taught by a lot of manifestation teachers. It so simple but very powerful. The premise is that before you get out of bed in the morning you play out your day in your mind. You break it down into sections, or segments and play each one as you intend it to happen.

You may have an interview for an important new work role and you spend the day prior to the interview worrying about what you're going to wear, trying to work out the best route so not to get stuck in traffic and arriving late and dishevelled. Wouldn't it be nicer if instead you spent that time visualising feeling amazing in your interview outfit, having a traffic free drive so you get there early and calm ready to answer each and every question thrown at you with ease.

That is segment intending, that's how easy it is.

There's a story that I like to tell when I am teaching on the reticular activating system and stepping into the life you want rather than the one you experience. My husband Steve has a belief that people here in New Zealand are bad drivers, he is constantly talking about the need to merge like a zip and the overall chaos that he sees on the road of bad drivers, no road signals, weaving in and out of traffic, sitting in queues and never being able to find parking spaces.

He carries that belief with him in his mind every time he goes out in the car so consequently that's what we see when he is driving. We see bad drivers, we never find parking spaces, we don't see people merging properly and more often than not there is a traffic queue of some description.

Now I, on the other hand, I don't have that belief and so when I go out I see good drivers, I don't get in traffic queues very often, I always visualize parking spaces before I even get to the place that I'm trying to go and so I always find a parking space, usually right where I have imagined it would be in my mind.

That just shows you the power of a belief that you hold, he thinks the experience won't be a god one, so it normally plays out how he believes it will and I have no such notion so I experience ease and flow, and parking spaces.

And so if you have a fear of anything and you're always fixated on the what might go wrong your reticular activating is going to show you all the things to prove that your fear is valid because, because as I have said previously, that's its job. And so with visualization, you can actually begin to reprogram the neural pathways in the brain even more because you are giving your brain powerful images of new feelings and showing it that you can actually have a totally different experience.

And so, visualization, even for just five minutes in the morning, spending time to carry out an intention of each segment of your day can have a great effect.

There's a famous study that was carried out by Dr Biasiotta at the University of Chicago where he split a team of basketball player's in to three groups and tested them on how many throws into the basket they could make. He asked the first group to go out and practice playing basketball for an hour a day as normal on the court, the second group he asked them to practice shooting the hoops for an hour a day but only doing it by visualising the practice, to not ever actually pick up a ball and throw it and the third group he had do nothing.

The study showed that the group who did nothing obviously had no improvement in the amount of baskets they were able to shoot. But the interesting thing is that the other two groups, the group that picked up the ball, went to the court and actually shot the hoops made exactly the same progress as the group who did nothing but visualise themselves shooting the hoops in their heads, they never touched a ball, they never took one shot in real life, it was all done using the power of visualisation and using their imagination to see themselves getting the baskets. So that proves the power of replaying something and doing something just by using your imagination and visualising it as if it is actually taking place in the real world.

There is an easy trick that you could do right now to prove to yourself the power of visualisation. I want you to hold out your and visualise a bowling ball being placed on it, its heavy, its weighing your hand down, you can feel it. Now change out the bowling ball for a tennis ball, it's a lot lighter, it's a lot smaller, you can feel the roughness of the outer coating. Now change your tennis ball into a gold ball, its tiny, it's dimpled, it's a lot smaller, its slightly lighter. That is the power of the mind, you could actually feel those things in your hand as if you were actually holding them.

You can practice visualisation in the way I have described above with the bowling ball, tennis ball and gold ball every single day to prove to yourself how you can change your perception of things just by visualising it. Then move on to your day and seeing it play out the way you want it too instead of the way you have always thought it would and then move on to changing your life by visualising yourself already having the thing you want, already living the life you want to live, already feeling the way you want to feel.

That is the power of the mind, that is how much control you can have over your own life if you just set yourself up to experience it before you have it in reality.

Take Away task:

I want you to try visualising. Pick something that you want to bring in to your life, how do you see yourself in your future vision, where are you living, how do you look, what are you wearing, what car are you driving?

I love doing this exercise with my clients because it allows them to see themselves, if only for the time of the visualisation, in a completely different world to the one they live in. This visualisation exercise allows you to step into your future and see yourself living the way you want to, feeling how happy you are, feeling and seeing how amazing you look and how confident you are.

Embrace this fully, it's a really positive thing to do.

See yourself on the flight that you normally hold fear over. Sit in the window seat, watch your favourite movie that's showing on the entrainment system, feel calm, feel excited that you are going on holiday, see yourself sleeping for some of the journey, writing in your journal maybe how lucky you are to be taking this trip.

The more you do this, the more you will trust that it works, the more you will see the things you are visualising coming to life in your reality. Proving to yourself that it works and making you feel better in the process.

Chapter Thirteen – Don't Make This Another Shelf Help Book

Before we go any further I want to ask how you are doing? Are you doing the take away tasks? Are you implementing the things I am teaching or are you reading this book and doing nothing?

I totally get it, this stuff is scary, even though you want to change and you want to feel better you are comfortable where you are and where you are is an easy place to stay BUT you picked up this book for a reason, you bought this book for a reason, you were led here, to me, to this book because you WANT to change.

We are all master procrastinators, which means that we intend fully to do these things but when the time comes to do the work we find all the excuses why we shouldn't.

I used to be one of those people. I would join free group after free group on Facebook, I would watch YouTube videos, I would read blogs and then I would go oh yeah, I know that, I know what to do, I'm good ....and then I would carry on with my life having all the techniques in my brain but I would never put into practice any of the things that I was being taught within those groups and within those trainings because I thought that I didn't need to because I thought that I knew more.

My thought process was totally in my ego at that point - I don't need to do that; I already know what these people are teaching me so I must be good already exactly as I am.

Do you want to know a not so well kept secret - my life didn't change, I didn't grow, I didn't evolve, I didn't get anything from any of those things because I was making all the things that I was doing shelf help instead of self-help, I would join the things and then shelf them, I would buy the books and shelve them, I would get the free PDFs or ebooks or the practices and then I would shelve them and I would never do anything with them, and because of that nothing in my life changed.

Nothing changed because nothing changed - I wasn't putting in the work however much I thought that I was, however much I thought I knew, I wasn't doing anything.

It was only when I got out of my own way and saw the value in what I was reading or learning or watching and decided to really implement it, when I decided to make a difference in my own life that's when the changes happened, that's when I began to see the synchronicities, to see the miracles, to notice the signs that my life was getting better and it happened from that point really, really quickly.

So my plea to you is this, do the work, implement the teachings, make the changes – to be honest it doesn't matter to me if you do this or not, you've already bought my book, you already have it in your hands right now reading these words that I have written. But my wish for you is that you get to see how amazing life can be, that you get to understand that you don't have to stay stuck, that you can change – I know because I did it and if I can do it then I wholeheartedly believe with all of my inner knowing that you can to, that is my wish for you.

I know what it feels like to be on the other side wishing for all the things that I have managed to achieve, I know how it feels to bully myself daily and I know what a difference I have right now, how much nicer my life is.

Take Away Task:

Don't shelve this book without doing anything, without implementing anything - I implore you, don't shelve it, use it.

You may find some of the things I talk about resonate with you and some don't, that's okay, find what works for you, find what feels good for you, even if it's only one thing, use it, don't read it and do nothing!!!!

Chapter Fourteen – Gratitude

I know what you're thinking, I know you've heard it all before, I know you think I am just another person going on about the power of gratitude. But what I want you to realise is that you hear this talked about, you see people discuss gratitude, you are asked to write a gratitude list by all the people you follow in the self-development space for a reason, because it works!!

Gratitude really does have the power to change everything, when you start to notice the things about your life that you love instead of the things that you dislike, you see more and more and more to love and less and less to dislike – that right there in itself, if you don't do anything else that I teach you in this book, has the power to be life changing.

The biggest tragedy that I believe most people experience in their lives is that when they are too busy, or too frustrated, or too sad, or too hyper critical of themselves and the lives they are living, chasing after all the things that they believe will make them happier, that equates to them never stopping long enough to notice that what they already have could be enough if they only stopped to really truly look at it.

True happiness is right here in all of our lives, we all have the capacity to feel it with just a little bit more gratitude for what we already have.

When you begin to practice gratitude it can be the start of monumental change. Gratitude is proven to have a positive effect on both your mind and your body, psychologically and physiologically.

Gratitude is not difficult but it does take practice and consistency, it's good to feel gratitude for a week and then stop, you will most definitely feel good for that week of practice, but it's even better to feel gratitude every day for the rest of your life. Your mental muscle is just the same as your physical muscles, they need to be worked consistently to see lasting change.

It's not a huge commitment either, just writing down five things that you are grateful for in your current reality paves the way for you to begin looking for more and more and more to be grateful for, more things to write in your journal, more things to show you that your life is already pretty damn good.

Try to be aware of your thoughts throughout your day, check in with yourself every hour or so and see if you can think of anything to be grateful for that might have happened. The more you do that the more you will start to flip around even so called negative situations and begin to see the lesson and the positive in everything.

So the most important thing here is to feel grateful, write a gratitude list, just 5 things, EVERY, SINGLE, DAY.

From there I want you to look back weekly at your lists and see what you have written, see what you have to be grateful for in your life, see all the little miracles that you experience every day, things that you may have missed and taken for granted before you start to see and really feel in this practice.

Start by feeling good for just the little things like a cup of coffee in the morning or a warm blanket on your bed during the cold winter nights and then as you get used to that and start seeing more things start to really ramp up those good feelings until it's almost impossible for you to feel nothing is going right for you in your life because where you once saw lack and judgement you now see gratitude and love.

The aim of all of this work is to rewire your brain to then start looking for more and more and more to be grateful for, eventually gratitude will become your normal state.

By rewiring the neural pathways in your brain to see good instead of bad, to be optimistic not pessimistic and to feel gratitude not to see problems this will begin to become imprinted in your mind, it will become a part of your every day and when you live that way, your reticular activating system will show you more and more things to make your life more enjoyable and before you know it you will be feeling better about everything, rather than seeing problems everywhere.

That's the beauty of this work, the loudest thought in your brain is always the one that you hear the most.

Being grateful shows you that your life has many good things in it already, things you previously took for granted, and your life changes without you really having to do anything else.

So let's start, right now!!!!

What are 5 things that you're grateful for right now, right at this moment in your life? Write them down and begin your gratitude practice.

Gratitude is something you must have before you can receive, it's not something that you simply feel after something good has happened. Most people are easily able to feel gratitude after something good has happened to them or they receive a gift but to really take advantage of the power of gratitude you have to become grateful before and after.

Be grateful for the things you already have, the small seemingly insignificant things that you take for granted, they are worth celebrating. The fact that you opened your eyes this morning and were given another day – that's something to be grateful for. You most probably opened your eyes in a comfortable bed, with blankets to keep you warm in a home where you feel safe, that's definitely something to be grateful for.

So I want you to think about this "What if you wake up tomorrow with only the things you are grateful for today?"

Looking at gratitude in that way evolved my practice from something I had begun to do on autopilot to something much, much more complex and evolutionary for me.

Sometimes even those of us that talk about and teach these principles are aware that to some people things such as gratitude lists can feel like a tick box practice. They can feel like you're going through the motions. They can feel like you're doing it because you're told to do it rather than because you want to do it. And that does not really come from a place of feeling but rather it comes from a place of doing.

What needs to happen to really allow you to tap into that gratitude and really make it evolve and change and have a massive difference in your life is to find the feeling behind it. When you can put feeling and emotion behind the things that you are doing on a daily basis that's when you see changes.

So, what if you wake up tomorrow with only the things you're grateful for today? Becomes what if you woke up tomorrow and you didn't have arms? Because he hadn't been grateful for your arms the day before? How would your life change? What if you woke up tomorrow and you couldn't see because you haven't been grateful for your eyesight or for your eyes? What if you wake up tomorrow, and you couldn't physically move? Because you haven't been grateful for the ability of your body to take the signals from your brain to move your arms, your legs, your shoulders, your waist, your entire body?

What if you woke up tomorrow and you could never ever see your husband again because you hadn't been grateful for him the day before.

On a less profound, but some might say just as important level, what if you wake up tomorrow and you can never source another drink of coffee ever because you haven't felt grateful for the ability to make a cup of coffee or buy a cup of coffee the day before? Doesn't that make the gratitude that you're going to feel much more powerful?

What if you wake tomorrow and because you'd had an argument with your children or they drove you mad, or they'd left cups on the coffee table instead of taking them to the sink the next day, suddenly they weren't there anymore? Wouldn't that make you appreciate everything about them and not just see the things that they didn't do when you asked them to tidy up?

What if suddenly, tomorrow that was all taken away from you because you hadn't been grateful for it today? You haven't seen the true value in the everyday in the mundane in the chaos in the simple, everyday things that you take for granted. So that quote, what if you woke up tomorrow with only the things that you were grateful for today has the capacity to take your gratitude practice to an atmospheric level. It has the capacity to totally change the way you see your gratitude list.

So when you are next asked to write five things you're grateful for instead of just going through the motions, doing it because you're told you have to with no feeling or energy behind it think of that quote. The emotion, the feeling, that's the power and when you can tap into that it's truly life changing.

Take Away task:

I want to share my own gratitude practice with you, the one that I have used every day now for as long as I can remember, the one that literally changed my entire way of looking at life.

Get yourself a notebook, go to the shop and buy something that you love, that you can feel grateful for (and you already have one thing right there to put on your list).

Take out your notebook every morning and write – the five things I am grateful for today are, and list them. The three people I send love to today are, and list them. How I want to feel today is, and write that feeling down.

Use the quote "what if you wake up tomorrow with only the things you're grateful for today?" as the catalyst for the feeling and the emotion behind this practice.

And then really look at the "how I want to feel today is" part of your new gratitude practice, and build on that.

Think of how you want to feel today and then create an affirmation around that feel good feeling and repeat it to yourself all day long as many times as you can.

In the shower, in the car sitting at traffic lights, doing the dishes, on the toilet even – use those snippets of time were you are not doing or thinking of anything else and say your affirmation.

For example, I want to feel happy could become "Today I choose happiness and I see it everywhere I go"

I want to feel loved could become "I am loveable, I see nothing but love for myself and everyone else today"

Chapter Fifteen – What Does Your Ultimate Dream Day Look Like?

One thing that has made the BIGGEST impact on my life is writing, or

more specifically dream day journaling. I have always loved writing but never really considered that writing could be the thing that would help me to live the kind of life that I wanted to live.

I knew that writing was a big part of me and a big part of my journey back from the brink to where I am today but it was only when I started to listen and tune in more to the internal nudges that I put two and two together and realised that writing about the future life I wanted to live could be just as therapeutic and inspirational as writing about my life, my past, brain dumping all my thoughts and feelings on a page and getting them out of my head in the traditional sense of a diary or journal.

When I finally listened to the nudges I understood that they were being sent to me by my higher self, by the universe, by my soul to make me write, to make me journal, to make me get it all out of my head and onto paper.

At first I just wrote down what I was grateful for (as I taught you in the last chapter) but then I took it one step further and began the scripting work that became the dream day diary process.

When I learnt about that I started writing with purpose, writing with feeling, writing with clarity and this is when the shift really happened for me. I started to write about what I wanted as if I already had it and the feelings behind the words became really powerful. I put in as much emotion as I could, used all of my senses and just allowed the words to flow onto the page.

The Dream Day that I began to envisage was the reality I wanted to create for myself. It wasn't about being on a permanent holiday but more about what I wanted to do with my life, where I wanted to live, who I wanted to be with, what I wanted to be doing as work, what clothes I wore, the car I drove, the environment I wanted to be in, how I felt about myself.

I have often been told in manifesting that you need to go big, the bigger the better, so in my dream day what I write about is the brightest and most abundant daily life that I possibly could live. I really go all out, I see myself there, I see the lifestyle, the work that I do, the people I touch, the house, the car, the everything.

When I teach this process to my clients I give them a few journaling prompts or questions to consider and think about. Things like, where do you live, what continent, country, suburb? In that dream location what does your home look like, one storey, two, is it a villa by the sea? How many rooms are there, can you see it, can you walk around it and picture your furniture, your belongings, your curtains, the wallpaper or paint colour, have you commissioned the services of an interior designer to come in and make it as beautiful as it could be or do you have an eye for design and a flair of your own that is buried deep down but that you can see when you walk around this house that you live in, in your future? Do you have a favourite room in your house, it could be your study, the kitchen, the lounge or even a sun drenched conservatory?

What can you smell, flowers in your garden, baking in the kitchen, your expensive perfume, vanilla from your essential oils that you use? What car is parked on your driveway, what colour is it, what make, what model, does it have leather seats or cloth? Can you feel your hands on the steering wheel?

And what about you, how do you see yourself? What are you wearing? What colour hair do you have, how amazing does your skin look, do you look happy, are you glowing? What are you doing and who is there with you, what food do you eat, what does your body look like, what is the weather like where you are in your dream life?

Then think about your work, what are your daily tasks, are you working from home or do you go somewhere? How many hours do you work, what do you earn, do you love your job, if you don't then pick again, think again – this is your dream remember, this is your perfect life, your perfect day.

How much money do you have in your bank account? How much family time do you have? What do you do when you are not working? Do you treat yourself and if so what to? How many holidays do you go on and where do you go? How does it feel to live this life? How has your life changed as a result of all this being your reality?

The biggest piece of advice I can give you is to go big, feel it, live it, see it, see, smell, feel, touch, be in the moment, be in the dream, make it vivid, use the skills you have already learnt in visualisation, put emotion behind it and really live it.

If you don't enjoy writing then you can dream day in your imagination, spend five minutes just thinking about and playing the scene in your mind's eye, be there, really live there for a few moments every day. Much like you would if you practiced segment intending, visualise your dream day instead.

You can dream day journal as many times as you feel the need, once a week, once a month or if it's a process that you enjoy and you feel the joy of writing it down and reading it back to yourself daily then do that. Those feelings, that joy, that is what will bring it closer to you, just by following a process that you find happiness in puts you in the vortex, energises you, makes you vibrate at a higher frequency – all of which allows you to manifest quicker and easier, which in turn makes you happy and isn't that the ultimate aim here, to be happier, to truly live in a better place with a better mind-set.

Would you like to hear about my dream day? The following passage is a snippet of one of my dream day scripts that I wrote. Over time you will find that your dream day changes, evolves, grows, just like you do, but hopefully reading one of my past days will give you some

idea of how much feeling, description and emotion to put in to it.

My Surroundings.......

I am sitting in my beautiful green, luscious back garden on The Wirral in England. I can hear the birds chirping in the trees and I can see the beautiful colours of the flowers that grow abundantly around me. I dropped the girls off at school and picked myself up my favourite coffee from the local cafe on the way home. As I sit now in my garden with the coffee cup warming my hands I feel so grateful that this is my life. We moved back from New Zealand over a year ago now and life has just got better and better.........

My House......

When we left NZ we sold all of our 3 rental properties and our own house which meant we got to come back and buy this gorgeous 4 bedroom home which also has a study which is my sanctuary and the place I record all of my YouTube content, write my books and my blog and work on my coaching business. It literally is everything I have ever dreamed of and the best bit is the money we bought home with us meant we don't have a mortgage. I finally have stairs again and get to go upstairs to bed, something I missed more than I ever realised I would when we lived in a one storey home in New Zealand.

My body..........

As for me my own health and well-being is massively improved here, I am happy and healthy, I don't worry about my body anymore, I eat good nourishing food which fills me with energy and I actually can't wait to get out of bed in the morning. All of the wasted years stressing about my weight has finally disappeared. I no longer want to be 55kgs and fixate on that number, I want to be healthy, to feel good in my own skin, to have energy to do the things I want to do and when I look in the mirror I see a confident, happy, content person looking back at me who actually looks better than I ever have at any stage of my life before.......

My work.......

I have a busy day ahead, but not so busy that it stresses me out. I wake up every morning and do a meditation and then some 'I know" rants to really get me pumped before I start my day. After school drop off I then get in to it with maybe a bit of yoga some days to get the blood pumping and a walk every afternoon before school pick up. Today I am recording a live video in my coaching programme for my amazing soul clients who I love showing up for and then this afternoon I will sit and write another chapter of my most recent book which I hope to have published before the year ends. It's been a year now since I launched my first coaching programme and it continues to go from strength to strength. I no longer hustle and spend hours a day working, I literally adore what I do and it all comes so easily, with so much ease and flow that I literally only have to work a couple of hours a day and I earn as much as I did when I was in stress and overwhelm..........

Take Away task:

Now it's your turn, create your dream day, feel it, see it, step into it, live it with all of your senses – be in the world that you dream about living.

How did that feel, read it back and fully embody the person you have written about.

Repeat this process as often as feels good to you. In the beginning I recommend once a week but when you are able to step into this person, this new life easily you don't have to do it that much because you will find yourself day dreaming in this life every day, imagining it without the writing process, being there, living it in your mind.

Chapter Sixteen – Believe

Do you truly believe that you can create everything you wrote about in the dream day process? That you can have anything and everything that you want to have in your life? Do you fully believe you have the power to change your mind-set and the way you see and talk about yourself?

Being in control of your personal power and really owning it all, the good the bad and the ugly, is essential in being able to make the changes that you want to make in your life. Once you truly believe that you can, you will achieve absolutely anything.

Wayne Dyer once said "If you believe it will work out, you'll see opportunities, but if you believe it won't, you will see obstacles" for me there has never been a truer statement spoken.

I was the same as you, I didn't believe in anything good, I wanted to and I truly thought I was doing all the right things but deep down in my subconscious, in my thought patterns, in the chatter that went on in my head I didn't believe any of it, I still had the negative cycle running the show and telling me all the reasons why I was useless and would never amount to anything. I was so caught up in that cycle I never saw what I had already achieved and what I had already accomplished, that didn't resonate with me anywhere.

The good news is that there are some really simple exercises that you can begin to practice to help you build your self-belief muscle. You may already be feeling better about yourself just from the work we have already done together in this book and by your carrying out the take away tasks, sometimes just reading the words I have written on the page and being in my energy can help but there is still more we can do to prove to you that you are amazing and you can change.

I want you to think about all that you have achieved already in your life, make a list if you want to. You may think that you haven't actually don't anything worthwhile, anything of note, anything to write home about but I promise you, you have - you just don't recognise it in yourself yet.

Did you finish school, that's an achievement. Have you bought a house, have you made that house into a home, that's an achievement. Do you have children, that is the most amazing achievement that you could ever do and the most important. Can you cook, even if its only beans on toast, do you hold down a job even if you don't actually enjoy it, it's still an achievement. Have you learnt to drive, lost weight, moved countries, they are all achievements that you may have done in your lifetime, they were all things I had done but never recognised as anything special, except they are special, all of those things.

Celebrate it all, really think about just how successful and amazing you are because that is the path to belief. I know I keep talking about the reticular activating system but remember its primary purpose is to keep you safe, to keep you where you are now, to keep you stuck – it doesn't mean to do it, it's not there to trip you up on purpose but think about it, all your life you may have believed that you are worthless, that you haven't achieved anything so your reticular activating system wants to make you right therefore it will show you all the reasons why you are right.

It doesn't want you to remember the things you've done well in the past, the achievements you have made - because then that would make you a liar and that's not what your brain wants to do.

It's our job, your job to overpower the old beliefs and forge new ones – think about all the things you are good at, dive deep, go through your entire life and pick off the achievements one by one. Show your brain that you are a success and it will have to show you more and more evidence that you are right because it doesn't want to make you a liar, that is how you gain belief, that is how you begin to see the world, your world differently.

Once you have completed your list of achievements read it back to yourself, feel the pride that comes with each and every thing that you have done no matter big or small, YOU achieved all of that!!!!!!

You did this, this was all you, really feel that.

Close your eyes and put your hands on your solar plexus (which is right above your belly button) and feel the pride in your body that goes along with these achievements, your achievements.

You have probably never taken the time to do this before, all of those things that you have done, that you have learnt, that you have achieved, they are truly special and they are where your belief in yourself will start so really feel it, know that you are a wonderful, incredible person who can do anything you put your mind to. This is your proof of that.

So we have already given your brain proof of what you have done for yourself but what about the lives that you touch every day too? Have you ever stopped to think about that, the difference and the value that you bring to others around you?

Are you a mum, a sister, a wife, a daughter?

Are you a dad, a brother, a husband, a son?

Do you serve people in some way for work?

Do you have colleagues who you help?

Do you have children who rely on you?

We all have an important role to play in the world and I am willing to bet that you have never taken the time to consider the difference you make to other people's lives.

You may be more focussed on the struggle (although by this point I hope you are making some big changes in how you view your world) than you are on the positives in your life. So today I ask you to really think about what you do for others, what ways you help others, what difference you make in other people's lives. Who relies on you, if you weren't there what would that mean for the people who are close to you? What value do you give to the world you live in?

It can be as simple as saying hello to a complete stranger that you met in the line at the supermarket, smiling at a mum who looks as if she may be drowning a little, letting her know you see her and you feel her.

Or it could be making sure all the bills are paid so you have electricity and heating or making dinner for your family. It doesn't matter, it's still making a difference in someone else's life. That's all you, you make that difference, you are the glue that holds it all together for a lot of people. You are important. So maybe with the words you have read above you can start to garner some belief in your achievements and how others see you.

But what about you, what about your own self-worth, your own self value. I am willing to bet that the way you view yourself is right at the bottom of the heap. For me when I was miserable and stuck I was so hyper critical of myself the self-worth I held for myself was non-existent and without that I had nothing no matter what I thought others may think of me.

What so you say to yourself over and over again on a none stop basis? What words are you using to describe yourself? Do you give yourself the same value that you give to others in your life?

SURVIVING TO THRIVING - A PRACTICAL GUIDE TO HELP YOU GO FROM BARELY LIVING TO LIVING WITH JOY

I have been teaching you to let go of the old belief's that are no longer serving you so now it's time to also let go of the critical thoughts, the way you talk to yourself and learn how to replace them with better ones, ones you come up with, with ease when you think about your children your spouse, your family, your friends even your pets.

Take Away Task:

I want you to get a piece of paper and draw a line down the middle of it so you have two columns on your page. Now make a list of all the critical things you say to yourself, both out loud or in your head, the critical negative chatter, get it all down on paper, you need to get it out of your head and truly look at it, brain dump it all.

My list would have looked something like this......

You are so stupid

You're too old

You're not pretty enough

Look at the state of you

Who do you think you are?

You're too fat

You are a terrible mum

You don't deserve to be happy

No-one likes you

Why would anyone love you

I wouldn't want to be your friend so why should anyone else

You are such a mess

You can't get anything right

You are the worst wife ever

Why would anyone love you

Can you relate? Do they sound familiar for you too? I want you to really look at the words you have written and now next to each one in the second column on you page you are going to write the complete opposite, flipping those beliefs on their head, every single one of them.

So my list would now become.......

I am clever

Age is just a number

You are beautiful

Look how amazing you are

I love who you are

Your body is the perfect just the way it is right now

You are an amazing mum

You deserve everything you dream about

There are so many people in this world who adore you

I love you

I would love to be your friend

You are amazing

SURVIVING TO THRIVING - A PRACTICAL GUIDE TO HELP YOU GO FROM BARELY LIVING TO LIVING WITH JOY

You are so good at so many things

You are a good, understanding and patient wife

Why wouldn't people love you

The second list is what you really are, it is who you really are if you were to ask your friends, your family, the people in your life who truly matter they would see the person on the second list, not the first. Read that list truly read it and take it in because that is who you are.

There are many ways to instil more belief into people but two of my favourites and two of the easiest ways are these, practice them whenever you feel you need a jolt of self-belief or confidence.

Do a "power pose, my favourite is the wonder woman pose - stand with your legs apart and hands on your hips and look up into the ski, feel the self confidence that gives you, or another favourite and one I get a lot of my less confident clients to practice is stand with your legs apart and stretch your arms up to the sky in a v shape and really feel the power that gives you.

Or just smile. Smiling is powerful, even if you have to fake it till you make it, just smile. In a *Psychological Science* study called "Grin and Bear It."[1] Which was carried in 2021 researchers placed chopsticks in the mouths of the individuals taking part to produce what is known as a Duchenne, or genuine smile, a standard smile or a neutral expression. What the study proved was that those in the genuine or standard smile groups had lower heart rates and were less stressed than the ones in the neutral expression group. Which proves that even if you don't feel like it smiling will make you feel better which in turn will instil more self-belief in you.

---

1. http://pss.sagepub.com/content/early/2012/09/23/0956797612445312

Pick one or pick both and practice them – the more you do them the more confidence in yourself you will feel and the more belief you will build for yourself moving forward.

Chapter Seventeen – Calm Mind, Calm Body

I remember the panic that I felt at different times during my life. When mum died the panic I felt was that of a child knowing how my life had changed but not really understanding how to deal with it or what it would really mean for me.

During my eating disorder whenever I felt I had over eaten or not purged enough, if I put on an outfit and felt fat the panic that I had gained weight would rise in my chest and almost strangle me.

During and after the earthquakes every time I heard the rumble of a lorry going past my home or an ambulance siren or a tsunami alarm warning me that a quake had happened out in the sea where I lived and to be aware of the need to move to higher ground the rising panic could and sometimes did literally floor me.

One of the most meaningful things that I can teach you is to slow down, to listen, to become more in tune with your body and its warning signs that you need to find a moment of calm. When you are in that hyper state of awareness it is so easy to forget all that you know. When you experience stress in your life and things begin to spiral out of control it is usually the bubble baths, the yoga, the walk outside in the sunshine, the reading of a good book, the things that you know to do to calm you, to relax you, they are the things that you stop doing because you perceive them to be unimportant or because you feel that you don't have the time.

So what do you do when anxiety strikes? If you are feeling a little anxious you can use some of the easy and quick techniques that I teach my clients, and use myself, to bring you back into your body and out of your mind. They are easy to implement and really, really work.

Anxiety has been a part of my life for literally years, so I have had to find ways to stop it in its tracks. It's kind of like that old friend who comes to visit sometimes but is kind of weird and you never quite know what to say to them.

When it strikes I feel it in my entire body. I know I'm not alone in feeling this way and I also know the world as we know it right now is not helping. 2020 and 2021 have proven to be extremely challenging for a lot of us but there are so many things that I know to do now when I feel the old familiar feelings rise.

If I am at home and in my own space I can recognise the signs and the symptoms. That's the time to practice self care, have a bath, meditate, journal, do some yoga etc.

Use your Tactile Senses - Touch something that feels nice and calms you such as a fluffy blanket, stroking your cat or dog, a cosy jumper or even warm water (a bath is amazing)

But what about those times when it comes on all of a sudden when I am out in public? When that happens I need something quick, something easy, something to ground me. Think about what you are wearing, feel the cuff of your sleeve or the edge of your jumper. What's in your handbag? Place a fluffy key ring or a stress ball in there, what about a rough, small stone, just something with texture. Feel it, squeeze it, focus on how it feels, hot, cold, soft, hard – this brings your mind back to the object and away from the panic.

Use your Sense of Smell, what scents do you love? What scents evoke loving memories for you? Chocolate, coffee, vanilla, lavender or one of my favourites from childhood, the scent of rain on a hot summer day. Activating your sense of smell is a great way to calm your body and bring your mind back to a different moment.

Smelling causes a quick reaction in the body, it helps relax or energise us, or even feel hungry or safe depending on what we are smelling. Imagine the smell of something in your mind. Find a scent that evokes a happy or comforting memory, maybe have a roller ball bottle in your car, or have a necklace around your neck with a smell pad enclosed in it, take your comforting smell with you wherever you go.

Use Positive Self Talk Phrases. Practicing positive self-talk such as I am safe, I am calm, I am okay, this will pass by, nothing upsets me today can calm your anxious mind quickly.

Pick a phrase that works for you in any given moment and repeat it like a mantra over and over until you feel the anxiety subsiding. Use this phrase as an anchor, this helps us to not get taken away in the wave of anxiety and instead anchors us back in the moment (as the name suggests). You could even try putting your name before it and stating something you know to be true, this tricks your brain.

"I am Jane. I am sat in my car, I am safe"

However, one of the easiest and fastest ways that you can press pause and calm your racing thoughts in any moment is just to simply to breathe.

Deep mindful breathing is enough to stop the fight or flight response your body wants to throw you into and will activate relaxation within your body instead. Meaning that your stress levels will instantly regulate and your mind will calm and no longer feel that feeling of being in danger which in turn returns you to a more balanced state.

Just two to three minutes of breathing with intent can calm your entire nervous system and it can be done literally anywhere, anytime. In the car, in the office, in the supermarket, and no one will even notice that you are doing it, except you.

The breathing practice that I am about to share with you is called geometric breathing, the first round of breath is about letting go of the fear and the rising panic that is taking over your body and mind and the second round of breath fills you up with love, with peace and with calmness.

All you do is inhale for five long calm breathes, hold for five long calm breathes and then let it go again with love for five breathes.

Practice with me now – consciously see your body letting go of the fear you are holding as you breathe in for 1, 2, 3, 4, 5 and hold for 1, 2, 3, 4, 5 and exhale for 1, 2, 3, 4, 5.

Now complete that round of breath again but this time imagine filling up your body with nothing but love as you breathe in 1, 2, 3, 4, 5 and hold for 1, 2, 3, 4, 5 and now exhale for 1, 2, 3, 4, 5.

During the first round of breathing feel in your body where you are holding on to the fear. We all have a place in our body where we feel fear, it can be in your gut, your heart, your head, your shoulders.

For me when I am tense I feel my shoulders hunching upwards towards the side of my head, and then I get headaches because I'm tight around my whole head and shoulder region.

There's always a warning sign that you need to relax, a place in your body that you feel it first, see if you can recognise that place in yourself the next time you are feeling stress or panic or overwhelm and consciously breathe into that space for five breathes feeling yourself letting go of the tightness, of the feeling in your body.

And then for the second round imagine yourself being filled with glorious golden light from head to toe. See it envelope your entire body, flowing in from a funnel at the top of your head and spreading its joy and its calmness throughout your entire being.

You may feel slightly dizzy at first when your practice this technique because your body will most probably be used to you breathing in erratic and short breath patterns.

Mindful breathing is one of, if not the best ways to bring your body back in alignment and make changes within your entire nervous system, just to breathe properly, inhaling and exhaling for the same amount of times can do wonders for you and your levels of stress, taking you from the flight or fight response to a calm and relaxed space within minutes.

What's more it can be used for everything. Stress, fear, situations where you feel anxious, panic, sadness or even just racing thoughts that flood your mind for no particular reason.

Have you ever had those nights where you are bone tired but the minute you close your eyes your brain wants to go back over every single minute detail of your day, criticising everything you did or didn't do and no matter how hard you try you just can't shut out the voices and get the rest you both need and deserve. This pattern of breathing will allow you to instantly let that go, to get out of your head and stop those spiralling thoughts and feelings from flooding your entire system.

Take Away Task:

Today's take away task is easy, just practice the breathing pattern that I have given you. Do it anywhere, do it when you feel stress, when your feel anger, when your feel overwhelm or even when you are lying in bed at night and just want to feel some calm come over your body.

The more you do it the more it will become second nature to you whenever you need it, whenever you feel anything rising in your body that does not feel good.

Chapter Eighteen – Self Love And Appreciating Your Body More

From reading the first part of this book you know that I struggled with weight issues throughout my life until I started to develop a habit of self love. I know that the two are intrinsically linked.

For me the self loathing started on the bottom step of that staircase as a 7 year old child losing her mum. Then began the rollercoaster of being an emotional eater, eating to feel better, berating myself for eating and then eating more to get over my berating myself. All the time spiralling deeper and deeper into self loathing.

I struggled with it for the majority of my life, bullied mercilessly at school for being overweight, feeling ugly and fat and worthless. And so began my journey to an eating disorder through my late teens and early twenties, losing more and eating less, telling myself I'll be happy if I can lose just a little bit more but never quite getting there. Exercising excessively and purging whenever I got the chance. Trying every diet under the sun, herbal, shakes, cabbage soup, detox, you name it I have tried them all, giving myself migraines for life when a particular diet pill I had bought disagreed with me right through to discovering that Andrews Liver Salts make a brilliant laxative!!!!

And then I got pregnant, that messed with my head so much that I was not sure how I was going to cope with putting on the necessary weight that I needed to deliver a healthy, thriving little baby. Being put under the hospital dietitians care at one point to keep an eye on me.

Then came the after effects of that, weight that I put on while being pregnant never quite going away, never allowing me to get back to the size I was before I became a mum, not being able to get back to doing the amount of exercise that I had been doing before as now I had a newborn to look after.

And so I ate less and less and less until I was fainting almost weekly and eating barely enough to sustain myself BUT never losing a single kg, unbeknown to me my body was in starvation mode, hanging on to every single calorie that I gave it and so never allowing me to lose anything. I was lost, I was miserable, fighting with myself every single day knowing that I needed to be a better role model to my two young impressionable daughters but not knowing where to start or what to do. I was pretty much at breaking point and I know this was the turning point, this was the dark day of the soul as people call it.

I had two choices, sink even further and possibly never come out or do something to change the way I felt and the way I was behaving. I had been learning about intuition and the law of attraction, I knew that it worked in other areas of my life so why not use it to help me in this one? Why not lean in to my intuition and ask the universe to help me, trusting that I would find the answer that I needed.

Once I did that and let go of the control I realised that I was overeating or undereating because of my emotions, my fear and my anxiety. It was a coping mechanism for me that I had used all of my life to hide away from the world, to have some kind of control when the rest of my life felt out of control. I realised I needed to use food to nourish and care for my body, not as a tool to punish it.

Staying overweight throughout my teens and early 20's was a protection method, if I was fat no one would look at me with love, therefore no one would get beneath the walls I had put up to protect my heart from being stomped on and broken once more, I knew that I could not take one more person leaving me, that would play into the abandonment issues that I had, the feelings of being not good enough and that everyone I loved would leave. So I stayed overweight and used food and self hate as my protective blanket.

It's truly brave to make changes from that place and if you are feeling like I did and hiding behind food as an emotional crux then I see you, and I need you to know that breaking free from that is truly miraculous. Seeing yourself through the eyes of love instead of hate is truly freeing.

And that is the trick to all of it, see yourself and more particularly your body differently. Your body is not just a body, it's the place that houses your soul. It's a place that houses your thoughts, your beliefs, your habits - everything about you that makes you, you. Being able to see myself as more than just what I looked like in the mirror for the first time was quite an eye opener for me. I was kind, I was filled with love for others, I had great empathy, I had an open and all-inclusive mind, I like to make people happy.

I liked so many parts of myself that were not my outer shell that once I began to actually think about that, I had the realisation that wanting to feel beautiful and striving to be thin and perfect to the outer world, wanting to ultimately change my outer shell was doing such and injustice to the parts of me what were on the inside. My personality, my love for all people, my humility.

For so long I had made my body out to be the enemy, I had compared myself to all of the so called perfect women that I admired, the perfect bodies, the beautiful faces, the women the media tells us every single day that we should look like and if we don't measure up then we're worthless.

But those women, those perfect bodies and faces, they are not real, they are what the media and big corporate entities use to sell their products and that brainwashes us into thinking that what we see each and every day is the norm. The truth is if you were to spend time in a room with those women you see as your ideal body shape, who you see as beautiful and perfect they too harbour doubts about how they look, about their features, maybe they feel too skinny, maybe they feel their legs are too long, maybe they struggle to fit in too.

And its time, as real women, that we celebrate not just our external but our internal. By doing that I realised that I was spending so much time in my own head, worrying, comparing, criticising, putting way too much validation on my looks and my size than on the person I was inside and what made me, me.

Have you ever stopped to think about how amazing your body is? level? How it knows what to do to keep you alive each and every day, to keep you, you? Our bodies are made up of billions of cells, each one working in harmony with the other to allow us to exist, each one working to allow us to experience life. Our cells need us just as much as we need them and when I really stopped to think about how cruel I was being to myself, how intolerant I was of those cells, how I put them down, how I took them for granted, how I hated them. I realised I was being completely and utterly disrespectful to the miracle that my body actually is, I was so caught up in the hatred of my outside that I never stopped to think about how incredible my genetic make up actually was.

The cells that make up all of our bodies see, feel, hear and experience everything that we do, so what message was I sending them, what hate was I throwing their way when all they ever did was keep me alive and functioning. I was abusing them daily both physically and mentally and I came to the realisation that if they felt everything I felt then if I continued to abuse them they would eventually fail.

I started to reach more and more for the things I am teaching you in this book like meditation and visualisation and going inward with exercise, doing Yoga and Pilates instead of punishing myself with a cruel and utterly soul destroying hard run on the treadmill. I used dance, laughter, playing with my girls instead of punishing aerobic sessions and movement that was utterly rooted in fear and blame, not in connection to my higher good and what I actually enjoyed to do.

I realised in the journey since then that food is to be enjoyed and if we use it and treat it the way it was intended then anyone can escape the bad thoughts and feelings and learn to love their bodies again.

Our intuition always knows what's best for us and if we throw away the control, the fear and the critical thoughts and just listen we always have the answers within us. Do what makes you feel good, eat in a way that nourishes your very soul and move in a way that brings you joy. If I can do this after all I have put my body through over the years than you can too. I understand better than most that it's a never ending journey and sometimes the demons catch me off guard and catapult me right back to where I started BUT I know that if I continue practicing self love I will always be one step ahead of the negative.

I used to think that one day when I reached a certain weight or let go of another dress size that I would finally be happy. If only I had the money for that botox, that breast lift, the lip plumping, the face lift, the liposuction etc, etc, etc. Over time however, I have come to realise that I was always loving myself, or striving to love myself with conditions attached. I was trying to mould my body into something that was not actually me. I needed to be a certain shape, have certain features, be a certain body type. Truthfully I was never going to get there because I had been born with a certain body shape and a set of genes that made me me and I was amazing just the way I was.

I learnt to stop comparing and stop living by the beauty standards that the world was throwing in my face everywhere I looked, I had to stop trying to reach for the unreachable, to be perfect - because the truth is perfect does not exist.

Learning to love me, truly love me, deeply love me, unconditionally love me is hard and it is a continual journey that I will forever be on. That love will not miraculously appear if I lose a few pounds, have a bit of botox or get a face lift - I had to come to the conclusion that yes those things might make me feel better momentarily but the feeling wouldn't last and I would then be back to square one, always striving for more because I would never quite reach that elusive so called perfection. True love is an inside job, it's a relationship that is cultivated and grows daily from the inside out, little by little, one realisation by realisation, step by step.

Throughout this book I have reiterated over and over that our brain just wants to keep us safe and show us experiences to back up the fact that it won't ever lie to us and so like in everything else I have talked about it will do everything in in its power to present to us experiences that match out thoughts and our feelings, and if you have spent years hating yourself, disrespecting yourself and criticising yourself you have created a very strong neural pathway in your brain which wants to keep you thinking and feeling the same way.

You have to work at the new relationship and the new thoughts and the new experiences and over time the new thoughts will become the more dominant ones and they will overpower the old negative ones and new neural pathways will be formed. You need to let go of what's no longer serving you, what truth be told NEVER served you. Create space in your life for the new you, fully embrace and embody the new you.

So I now invite you to go deeper, to reconnect with your cells, with your internal make up, with yourself on a cellular level - don't ignore them, don't criticise them, don't hate them, show them love and appreciation for without them your body would not function.

If you are not sure how to do this use my example below:

I am thankful to my body, to my strong legs which carry me where I need to go every day. My eyes, which allow me to see me favourite people, watch my favourite films and read my favourite books. My ears, which give me the power of music and let me listen to my favourite songs, the sounds of nature and the laughter of my children. My internal organs, which take care of everything automatically so I

can focus on my world outside. My taste buds, which let me truly enjoy my favourite foods. The lines on my face and the stretch marks on my body that remind me I have lived and which show the map of my life. My scars both internal and external which give me the honour of knowing that I am a survivor. Thank you for everything you do for me, I love you.

Repeat that mantra to yourself daily and watch your relationship with your body change.

Take Away Task:

Write a letter to your old self, express all the feelings that you have towards it, tell it how you are not that person anymore, take away its power and then either rip the letter up or burn it in a safe place to symbolise that you will no longer tolerate the old you, the old patterns, the old thoughts. But most of all decide today that you will love yourself from this day forward, make yourself a priority in your life, be your own best friend, do not talk to yourself like an enemy anymore. Do not tolerate it!!!

I fully believe that every single person deserves self love, deserves to feel happy, deserves to feel nurtured and to inhabit a body that they love. Make that your priority today and every day of your life moving forward.

Chapter Nineteen - Meditate

I honestly believe that the secret to changing thought patterns, beliefs, desires, even feelings come from a place deep within us. We all have the capacity to have the life of our dreams we just don't know how to tap into it at will.

For me the easier I get in the 'zone of abundance' as I like to call it, the faster everything flows to me and the quicker changes in my life occur.

My secret for getting into the zone of abundance is meditation.

I have a deep seated knowing that when we are disconnected from our inner being, from source, from ourselves we feel stuck, we feel stagnant and we feel despondent. These feelings of lack are just a symptom of disconnection. In my life today I welcome these feelings because they are a reminder that whenever I feel down or begin to feel something strange and not welcome in my mind and body that is my warning sign, that is my intuition guiding me back to myself, showing me that I am becoming disconnected and that I may have let some of my techniques, the ones I am sharing here within this book, lapse.

Life is happening all around us and we all forget how to feel grateful and get stuck in a rut on occasion but now when those feelings begin to build in me I know the fastest way out is to get into the 'zone of abundance'

Meditation is something that I pushed away for the longest time. I knew all the reasons why I should meditate and had read countless studies on how good it was for not only my mind and mind and body connection but also for my inner being and my ability to listen and interpret messages being given to me to help guide me on my path.

I have always had a very active imagination, which for visualisation and imaginary work is a wonderful thing, but in the case of meditation this can and has caused problems many times for me. As hard as I tried I always found it impossible to shut off my thoughts, empty my head and sit with nothingness. So countless times meditation was put in the too hard basket.

But something kept drawing me back, like a whisper of knowing telling me to just give it one more try, and so I did, googling ways to meditate, how to meditate properly, what to do if you can't meditate. From that I found guided meditation, and from that I discovered deep breathing meditation, both practices that I have followed from that point forward with massive success.

With guided meditation I find it easy to follow along to someone's voice, to listen to words of encouragement, giving me instructions, guiding me. Instead of allowing my thoughts to infiltrate my quietness I listen instead and by concentrating on the words being spoken I find my brain does not want to but in with words of its own quite so much. I enjoy guided meditation so much I have devised meditations of my own and quite often will listen to my own voice giving me the instructions, as I said previously in chapter nine your own voice is the most powerful voice that you can listen to and so doing this heightens the experience even more. It's not necessary for you to do this however, not yet, not ever if you don't feel called to. Listening to others can be just as potent.

With breathing meditation I find I can go even deeper and get to the zone even quicker. I find it easy to simply close my eyes and focus on my breath. The sound of my inhaling and exhaling, feeling the whisper of my breathe in and out of my mouth or nostrils as I go. Yes sometimes thoughts will find their way in to my quietened mind nut the more I practice this the easier I can send those thoughts straight back out again on an exhalation.

I like to practice earth breathing which is when you breathe in and out through your nose, but there is also air breathing where you breathe in and out through your mouth. Pick the one that feels good to you and just breathe for 15 minutes each and every day in silence to reap the massive rewards of this practice.

There are numerous studies that back up the benefits of meditation in some form or others but simply put, your brain in day to day will be functioning at what is called beta cognitive level. You can at times if you are particularly mindful and present, like an athlete for example, function at what is known as the gamma level. When you begin to relax and quieten your mind, either in meditation or at night as you are drifting off to sleep, your brain will progress in to alpha level. This is where you are open to suggestions and therefore is an optimal time to get creative and do your visualisations or personal affirmations to attract what you want to you. But as you go even deeper your brain will move into the theta level and this is the depth you can reach and where you can tap into your intuition and guidance through a daily meditation practice.

So just imagine how your life could change and how you could attract everything you dream about if you decided from this day forward to meditate for 15 minutes each day as you are drifting off to sleep when your mind naturally wants to slip down the levels into alpha and theta easily.

And then think about how you could perhaps go one step further by doing it again in the moments you wake, before you are fully aware just for five minutes, breathing with earth or air breathe consciously and with intent.

Meditation to me is purely about releasing resistance, tuning in to guidance and opening yourself up to see beyond your current circumstances and allowing your mind to show you and give you answers to sometimes unspoken questions.

Creating a meditation practice and sticking to it allows space for miracles beyond anything else I have ever experienced because when we learn to stop our over thinking thoughts and realign back to ourselves we can access diving intervention, we can stop the chaos and the feelings of overwhelm and actually see and hear solutions.

Take Away Task:

I want to encourage you to start a meditation practice. It does not have to be the full 15 to 20 minutes that I have explained above if that feel too hard or too much of a stretch for you right now. Sixty seconds of any type of meditation is better than none and you will be amazed at how much better you can feel in such a short time. Less anxious, less overwhelmed, less worried.

You could practice one minute of breathing meditation and build up to fifteen as it gets easier and becomes more second nature to you. Other types of meditation to try could be a guided meditation or maybe try fire meditation, by looking at a candle or any open flame as you sit. This allows you to be in the moment and clears the mind. Fire is a powerful element for cleansing and so works especially well. Or you could try a mantra meditation where you repeat a certain word or phrase over and over again either aloud or silently as you sit quietly. The word you chant is used as a way to focus your mind and stop your thoughts from taking over.

Just start, commit to a meditation practice and build the time up as you go.

Chapter 20 - Feel It To Heal It

I want to touch on the vortex of emotions, the range of feelings, low to high, that give us a guide for where we are in any given moment.

When I first began doing these practices for myself, on myself, I carried a copy of the guidance scale with me in my bag and saved on my phone. Doing this allowed me to see at a glance exactly where I was and what I had to work on in any given moment. Nowadays with anyone I work with I recommend they do the same, it's a powerful thing to have a visual of your feelings instantly.

For the majority of this book I have been talking about the importance of being happy, being mindful and being in charge of your emotions, having hope, living in love, having excitement, feeling joy and abundance. These are all feelings that we should strive for in our life and are all on the top end of the guidance scale.

But we are human right?

And humans have emotions and as humans we don't always have good emotions. There are times when we feel those lower end feelings. We get stuck in frustration and jealousy and anger and sadness and lack.

These are all feelings that any manifesting teacher or mindset coach will tell you that you don't want to feel. I hold my hands up, I am one of them, I know I've said that many times before in this book, on my YouTube channel, on my podcast, anywhere that I can that you want to get out of those feelings and get back to living at the high end of the vortex.

But, as I've said we're human and as humans we are going to have days when we're down, that is inevitable, I truly do not believe that anyone is being authentic, honest or true to themselves if they don't feel sadness, or lack or anger or fear at least some of the time.

The problem with life is that as we grow up somewhere along the journey to adulthood we come to the conclusions that negative emotions are bad and that we should avoid them at all costs.

You may have early memories as a child of being told to stop crying, you're being too emotional, it's embarrassing, there's nothing to be afraid of, stop being silly and so many more. So in hearing those statements you have probably internalised the notion that too many emotions can be a bad thing, that anything unpleasant is actually not an acceptable thing to feel. And so from an early age you learnt to supress your so called bad feelings, to shove them deep, deep down and pretend they weren't there.

The problem with this way of thinking however is that you then become unable, or unwilling, to feel the hard or low thoughts and feelings, and so you come up with many ways of not experiencing them. This then becomes a control strategy and that in itself is unhealthy – in the words of Elsa, conceal don't feel, don't let it show.

Keeping such tight control of your emotions then ultimately becomes the issue and causes you more harm than good. Suppressing or avoiding the hard feelings creates more distress in your body and therefore stays with you for much longer and can cause long term issues both mentally and physically. It comes back to the well-known saying - what you resist persists.

The trick with all emotions is to feel them fully, to let them in, acknowledge them and then let them pass, ride the wave but don't stay on the wave.

Acknowledging the feeling, giving the feeling a name and a reason to be in your body and in your mind can actually teach you a lesson. Feelings are sent to us for a reason always, we feel feelings to tell us something about ourselves, both good and bad.

Letting go of controlling your feelings can be really scary and frightening, I know this from personal experience, but what I can also tell you from personal experience is that ultimately your happiness totally depends on your being willing to accept and let in the emotions that bring you discomfort just for a little while. Doing this allows you to process them, get them out of your body and let them go, again in the words of Elsa.

Keeping your feelings within you, supressing them, closing them down, allows the feeling to fester and to grow, you do not want that to happen, ever.

When you learn to stop running from your pain and let it in you can feel it to ultimately heal it, you can prove to yourself that you're strong enough to survive what you have been supressing, and that brings in a level of freedom that you may never have felt before.

What you then learn is that in many cases you can use your pain and your negative feelings to your advantage, because feelings, both good and bad, always leave clues to what we truly want out of life.

To give you an example of where feeling lower end feelings can be useful let's take a look at jealousy. If you are feeling jealous of someone or something that someone has, that is a clue to what you want even if you don't realise it.

You see that Kate down the road has got herself a brand new car and every time you see her driving it, or every time you pass her house and it's sitting on the driveway instead of going oh my god look at that amazing car instead you go to jealousy and you think something along the lines of "what a bitch, she's got such a cool car and she doesn't even deserve it, I should be driving something like that not her, she has literally got so many nice things, why can't I have that for once. Look at my old banger. I want her car, I could never have a car like that, I can't afford it, and it's so unfair that she can".

That voice in your head, the chatter that just called Kate a bitch and told you that you don't deserve a car like that one, actually, if you look behind the jealousy and you look at the feeling and the emotion behind the jealousy that is telling you that you want her car and that you are not satisfied with your own car. So therefore what you can do in that moment is question where it comes from. So I'm feeling jealous because she's got this brand new car, does that mean I want that car? Does that mean I'm not happy with my car? Does that mean I need to up level my car?

And so if you look at why you're feeling the feeling, why you are reacting the way you're reacting it can tell you something about your own life where you may be feeling lack. So then you can start to question that feeling even more, dig deeper in to why that jealousy has risen in you and what that means going forward.

In this case with Kate and her car you could put a picture of that car on your vision board, you could start dream day journaling about that car, you could start doing some affirmations about the car you want to have on your driveway, you could start doing the work to bring your energy into alignment with the car you want to drive. You could go to a dealership and you could test drive one and feel your hands on the wheel and start to visualize yourself inside that car. All of those things bring the car into your energy field, into your conscious and subconscious mind and start to lead you towards maybe having that car one day for yourself.

So you can use the jealousy, you can use the snarky remarks that you may have said about Kate down the road in her brand new car and you can use that because that jealous feeling gives you clues as to what you want.

You might see somebody on television, you might see a famous person who's earning so much money, they have got this amazing career, the lifestyle you want to live, the house, the partner, the clothes, the career, the fame, the money and you feel such overwhelming jealousy that you call this person all the names under the sun, you can't watch them on the TV, you are critical every time you open a magazine and they are in it, you can feel your heckles rising every time someone even mentions their name. The reason why you called them all the names under the sun, the reason why you feel jealous is because they have something you want, so ask yourself what part of the lifestyle this person leads do I crave, what am I jealous of exactly? Is it the fame, no, is it the clothes, not really, is it the partner, no I'm happy with mine, is it the luxury lifestyle, the abundance of money.... Ah there it is, that is what I feel I am lacking in my own life, that is the clue to what I want to bring into my own field of vision. It's not the person, it's what you perceive they stand for or they have that you want. Feelings always leave clues.

I can remember in my own life before I had written and published my first book it was something I had always wanted to do. It had been a dream of mine for the majority of my lifetime, even when I was young and had no clue what I was going to do with my life, writing had always been something I was good at. I would see friends in my social media world on Facebook bringing out books, publishing memoirs, writing poetry, becoming published authors and my mind would instantly go to that place, why would anybody want to read a book on that? Why have they written a book, they don't have the experience that I have, I could do that so much better. But then I would catch myself and ask why was I reacting in that way, why was I negative?

Normally when I see someone becoming successful I am happy for them, I genuinely feel happiness that they are living out their dream, because I know there is always enough for all of us, if they can do it that means it's possible, if they can be successful in this realm that means I can be successful too, if they can have that thing they are showing the world that actually anyone can.

So by my getting dragged down in the lower end feelings, in the jealousy I knew that it was because I felt so strongly about the book writing, the being a published author that I wanted it for myself. And in that knowing I could do something about it. I could put it on my vision board, I could visualise the front cover, see myself holding it in my hands, and then do the work to make it a reality. Actually write it, research publishers, would I sell on amazon alone or other book stores, and the more I did that, the more excitement I felt about it and the more I aligned myself with it and made it happen.

So however much we try and stay in love and joy and excitement and all of those good feelings, which is where we want to reside most of the time, if we find ourselves feeling jealous, angry or feeling sad or cynical or giving criticism to something we can use those feelings to our advantage by asking why, why is that particular thing having an impact. We can use the anger, the frustration, the jealousy, the sadness, the fear even to lead us further down our own path, to show us where we still need to grow, to show us our next right step, to up level into our next phase of growth. Those feelings show us where we have a perceived lack.

So in my case I had the car, the house, the career, the freedom business but feeling anger and jealousy over someone writing a book, there was my next step, there was my clue to what I wanted to do next. That was my growth.

Take Away Task:

Explore the low level feelings, dig deep into why you feel low, journal on them, think about them. Ask yourself some questions about why are you feeling this jealousy? Why are you feeling this anger, why you are feeling this sadness or frustration?

Feelings always lead us to the root cause, to something that we potentially want or something that we need to do to lift ourselves out of the gloom and up the guidance scale of emotions.

Feeling your feelings, both good and bad, allow you to step up and continue to create the magical life that you want for yourself.

Emotions are good, both top and bottom emotions. You have to feel feelings, you are a human being and as a human being you are given emotions daily.

Learn to use them to your advantage, rather than getting dragged down into the pit of despair and staying there, question what they are trying to tell you because once you realise where the jealousy is coming from or where that anger is coming from or where the negative talk about that particular person or thing is coming from, you can use it and you can pinpoint what it is that you feel you haven't got yet.

That is true freedom and true growth potential.

Chapter 21 – Don't Judge A Book By Its Cover

Everyone has a certain style of love language, both for themselves and others. I jokingly refer to my love language as doing Pilates, eating peanut butter and drinking a good barista made cup of coffee. I love Pilates, it makes me feel good and strong, I will literally sit and eat the peanut butter out of the jar and coffee is just my thing. It's no secret in my world that I have to have a proper barista made coffee every single day, instant just does not cut it. I know that maybe sounds pretentious to some of you and I do realise how lucky I am that I get to do that and I am extremely grateful that I'm able to go and buy myself a coffee every single day without fail.

Those are three acts of self love that I do for myself daily but they got me thinking about the things that we do for ourselves and the things that we don't do for ourselves, that then led me to really look at my life from an outside point of view.

If you look at my life today, and if you'd have looked at my life 25 years ago, they'd look pretty similar. You would still have seen me eating well, you would see me choosing salads over chips. You would see me exercising daily. You would see me going to get my hair done, you would see me trying to get a good amount of sleep, you would see me not drinking alcohol.

Side by side my life would look very similar but the difference internally, the difference from a place of love and acceptance and growth and love language and all of those unseeing things could not be more different.

Back then 25 years ago I would eat healthy but that was restrictive. It wasn't because it was what I wanted to do from a place of love. It was because I felt I had to do it from a place of hatred. I would exercise the same as you would see me doing that today. I could be moving my body in some way, taking a weights class or doing Pilates at home with my phone and an app, I do that today because I love it and because I enjoy it and because it exhilarates me but I did it back then because I felt I had to, because I felt that I would never be perfect or thin enough or fit enough or toned enough or any other kind of enough. And it was from a complete lack of love. It was from an absolute place of hatred.

I have my hair dyed once every seven weeks because it makes me feel good and because I don't ever see myself with grey hair because that would not feel like me, whereas back in the day 25 years ago, I would have had my hair done to look a certain way that was perceived to be acceptable to me and to how I thought others saw me. It wasn't about the feeling. It was about what it looked like. What image was it portraying?

I remember having my eyebrows tattooed about seven or eight years ago but I didn't tell anybody I was doing it, my ego told me that it was vain and people would judge me. I actually had them done and then covered them up with makeup because I was so worried about the image that I was portraying to the world. What did that say about me the fact that I felt I was vain enough and that I needed to go and have my eyebrows tattooed. You know what, if I have my eyebrows tattooed today, it would be because it would be making my life easier because then I wouldn't have to draw them on every morning and I would not care less what people thought. I would be doing it from a place of love for myself and have total acceptance of it making my life easier.

And so today when you see me eating salads, when you see me choosing something healthy off the menu as opposed to going for the fries. I'm not doing that because I'm scared of the amount of calories that I put in inside my body. Although, if I'm totally honest, I still have those feelings. I don't think those feelings will ever go away completely because it's a part of me. It's part of my history. It's part of my journey. It's been a massive part of my growth. And I am a girl who had an eating disorder - but that doesn't define me anymore because I refuse to let it.

These days for the most part I exercise and eat healthy because it's what I choose to do from a place of love rather than doing it from a place of absolutely hating my body. For absolutely hating myself with such a passion that it fuelled my entire day, that I literally counted every single calorie and I panicked if I ate something that I perceived to be bad.

It was Mother's Day not long ago and you may have seen on my social media that I had a piece of carrot cake because I love carrot cake. It's my absolute favourite dessert in the entire world and so I went out for coffee and cake with my girls and I thoroughly enjoyed my piece of carrot cake and it came from a place of love, I wanted to do it. It made me feel good and it tasted amazing.

Compare that to the days when I only allowed myself to have cake on Christmas day and on my birthday. And even then I would have that piece of cake then go to an exercise class for three hours to get rid of it because I felt so guilty that I'd eaten the so called bad or empty calories.

And so I wanted to just point out that sometimes you can look as though you have complete self love for yourself. You can look as if you're eating the right foods. You can look as if you're exercising and being healthy. You can look as though you're taking care of yourself by having your hair done or having your eyebrows done or having your nails done but that can be so very different from one person to the next.

One person can do those things because they love how it makes them feel. They love what it does for them. They are totally blissed out by the feeling of taking a Pilates class or going for a run. Whereas somebody else can be doing those very same actions but it's from a place of such deep hatred and total lack of self acceptance and lack of self love that it is festering on the inside.

On the outside, to the outside world, to the people looking in it looks entirely the same but internally it's so very different.

I do have an addictive personality. I recognize that in myself now, I'm definitely an all or nothing type of person. So the Pilates class I do today is to make me feel and look amazing from a place of love for my body and what it can do for me, and does do for me. Compared to when I exercised back in the day as a way to feel some control. As a means to an end, a way to restrict calories and to keep my body burning, to keep my metabolism high, all from a complete and utter lack of self love.

The acts may be the same but the feeling and the motivation behind them could not be more different.

I may not be as thin as I was back then but do you know what? It's not about that for me anymore. It's about how I feel and how healthy I perceive myself to be in my body and how much I love that.

Take Away Task:

I want you to take some time today to think about where are you doing things for yourself that come from an act of love, as opposed to an act of shame.

That contrast, my life looks the same, I'm doing the same things but I'm doing them for such totally different reasons and the feelings I get from them are so totally different.

I might go for a run on the treadmill once a week now but that's because I choose to not because I feel that I have to, that I'm lacking something or that I'm not good enough.

There is such a difference. I want you to be honest with yourself, get real and raw.

Where are you carrying out acts of seeming love for yourself but they're not coming from a place of love. Where are you pushing yourself from a place of contrast and hardness and lack when you should be coming at it from a place of love?

What are you doing in your life that you think is from a place of love, but actually it's not. It's actually from a place of no self-respect or lack or hate even, like I was back in the day.

It's very vulnerable to get that that clear with yourself sometimes and to realize where you are doing certain things that aren't coming from a place of good or a place of self respect. That may be coming from that place of image or what you want to portray or what you feel you have to do or have to be like, as opposed to what you actually love.

Today's practise is don't judge a book by its cover, don't look at somebody and think that they have an abundance of self love or fall in to comparison.

Those things you see, the things they want you to see could be coming from a complete and utter lack of self respect as it was to me back in the day.

Chapter 22 – Momentum

My journey wasn't easy, learning these principles and implementing them, especially in the beginning when I had absolutely no way to know if they worked and nothing to show for them, was tough. There were days I found it hard to get out of bed and drag myself through the day never mind write my gratitude list and meditate for 20 minutes.

Working with others now it's also a question I get asked a lot, how I kept going even through some of the toughest times – the answer I always give, small, baby steps, taking one day at a time until those small steps equal massive shifts which cause momentum, and once you have momentum that's when things get easier.

In the mindset and coaching sphere there are definitely buzz words. If you are in the space of personal development or you follow certain teachers or even influencers, you will have come across the term quantum leaping. It's literally all over my Facebook and Instagram feed.

All the posts that I see are about quantum leaps, do this and you will have this quantum leap, this massive breakthrough and this quantum leap will take you to this new timeline or this new thing and I am here to debunk that myth. So what exactly is quantum leaping and timelines and how do I have one if I don't even know what it is?

I for one don't like buzzwords I think that things need to be in plain English. Because we're not all coaches and we're not all experts and we don't all know what a quantum leap actually means.

And so I want to break it down and I want to make it slightly easier, slightly more understandable, and actually let you know that you're all making quantum leaps, no matter how small or how big and that leads to momentum.

A lot of you who have been here with me from the start, you will know that I began my journey back to me by joining a network marketing business. I was in a makeup selling company, that decision sent me on the trajectory to getting into the coaching space, learning about mindset, researching the brain, the subconscious and the conscious, learning about the reticular activating system, completing training in LOA, NLP, Life Coaching, energy work and everything else I now teach and share.

What a lot of people looking in to network marketing from a place of judgement and ego don't realise is that one of the success principles in network marketing is personal development. So by making that seemingly insignificant decision to join my first company I began to learn about mindset changes, how doing a little bit of personal development each day, from reading a book like this one or watching a video or listening to a podcast, had the capacity to change my mind and alter the neural pathways in my brain.

One of the books that I read back then was called the compound effect. It basically says that success in anything does not come from these huge, huge steps. It's not the big things that we do in our life, the so called quantum leaps, that make the success. It's not the big huge action steps, it's not the drastic changes. The success actually comes from the compound of seemingly insignificant small tiny baby steps that we take every single day that we don't even realise we are taking.

So this phrase quantum leaping to me is not helpful and does not ring true. I don't like it because I don't want you to think that if you're not out there making these massive, drastic breakthroughs every day, that you're doing something wrong, that you're not going to get to where you want to go or that you're not going to have the success that you see other people having.

SURVIVING TO THRIVING - A PRACTICAL GUIDE TO HELP YOU GO FROM BARELY LIVING TO LIVING WITH JOY

You may see another influencer or author or tedx talk and to the outside world looking in it seems as if this new hot thing popped up overnight and came from nowhere. Now they have got this massive raging success, literally from nothing obvious, from doing no obvious work.

But the thing that you don't see, the thing that you can't know is that even though they may have done that one thing, that one live event or that one book or that one YouTube video that enabled them to find success, there will have been tiny, tiny baby steps in the background compounding, getting them ready, bringing them to the forefront, teaching them.

There's an image that comes to my mind of an iceberg, and it's one that is put in network marketing groups all of the time, and it's literally the tip of the iceberg sticking out of the water. We see the small part that is the top, the tip of the iceberg, but what you don't see under the water is all of the failings and the following and the learning and the stepping out of the comfort zone and the trying something new. Launching to crickets, trying to build to nothing and the unsuccessful sales that all come underneath the water. The bottom part, the bit of the iceberg that you can't see, the bit where there's been pain, the bit where there's been learning, the much larger part.

All of that, the good and the bad, it compounds and compounds and compounds up to this big leap. To the success, to the part that people actually see and recognise.

For me and my own personal experience, the breakthroughs didn't come from one meditation, or one book or one TEDx talk, or one journaling session, it's been the hundreds, sometimes 1000s of meditation sessions, of breath work sessions, of energy sessions, of Reiki treatments that have come before that which have all compounded one on top on top on top of the other.

It hasn't been that one thing that tipped me over into the success realm. It's been the tiny steps, the hundreds of tiny things that I did prior to that that caused the breakthrough.

So can you see it's not just about doing that one thing, it's about consistency. It's about the showing up day after day, doing the work even when you don't feel like it, when it's hard, when it hurts. When you feel like you're getting it wrong, when you feel like you're trying to put a square peg into a round hole. It's the showing up anyway. It's consistently doing 20 minutes of meditation a day, one video a day, one podcast a day. It's those little insignificant, tiny, tiny steps that compound over time that lead to the success.

One day of journaling won't change a mindset. One spoken affirmation won't rewire a neural pathway in your brain. It's the hundreds of times you say that affirmation that rewires the pathway and drowns out the old belief and forms the new one. It's not one thing. Its hundreds of tiny things that become the quantum leap in disguise.

For me doing this, sitting here now and writing about what I've learned on my journey. This happened by me sitting here and typing one word on my keyboard, pressing play and speaking one word, doing one recording for my YouTube channel, making one podcast episode at a time, one at a time, on top of each other.

It's the little things that I have done over the years that have taken me out of my comfort zone.

It's all those little insignificant, tiny decisions from being a career coach in the first place, to deciding to not go back to work and be a stay at home mom to joining that network marketing company to reading my first personal development book to doing my first post on Facebook to selling my first bit of makeup to learning that I loved this side of it and not the sales side that led me to here, to writing this book.

SURVIVING TO THRIVING - A PRACTICAL GUIDE TO HELP YOU GO FROM BARELY LIVING TO LIVING WITH JOY

So I want to remind you that those quantum leaps, those big decision come from tiny steps. And those tiny steps can lead to huge success.

Somebody that you may follow on Instagram that has millions of followers, they started with one follower, just like everybody else. Somebody you might see on Facebook that has a major following, they started by getting one friend and doing one post just like you could, somebody who has written a book and become a best seller, they started by writing one word, one sentence, one chapter at a time.

The little insignificant decisions, the times you listen to your internal nudges to do something, the inner guidance that you learn to follow they are what make the huge quantum leaps that make the big drastic action.

So I want you to remember when it feels hard, when it feels like you're not getting anywhere, when it feels like you're doing all the things and nothing is changing believe me changes are being made.

It is a series of tiny, tiny, tiny steps in the right direction that lead to the big shifts that lead to you getting where you want to go. Those little tiny steps they all build on each other one decision at a time deciding to trust your intuition. One meditation at a time, one book at a time, one podcast at time.

Progress can come out of the smallest steps.

So decide now, how badly you want to change your life, how badly do you want to change your life, your energy, your dreams, your day to day? Because those tiny steps build momentum.

Momentum is truly a universal gift because the more energy you put into something the more you get back in return. And the more you keep putting in the faster it gets.

To give you a simple example about momentum let's look at a car, it starts to move from nothing, then it gets going and the wheels turn faster and faster and suddenly its travelling at 100 miles per hour with consistent energy applied to it, it keeps going and it gets faster and faster. And that same principle can be applied to you changing your life for the better.

The more momentum that you put behind what it is that you want, the more you focus on it, the more you keep yourself in the upper levels of the emotional guidance scale, the more you follow the principles I have talked about in this book, the more momentum you will get.

You already know how to use momentum in your life because it's taken momentum to get you to where you are now, feeling stuck and hopeless. Because momentum can go down as well as up. If you have been continually thinking about all of the bad things, all of the lack in your life, all of the things you want to change then that breeds momentum downwards, that leads to the black hole, to the constant negativity, to the crisis that you may now find yourself in.

Which is why it's so important that we guide our thoughts in the right direction, up the guidance scale, not down it. The longer your thoughts stay positive, the stronger they become, the longer your thoughts stay thinking about your dream life, the louder that thought becomes in your brain.

The processes that I have been teaching you over the course of this book are designed to make you feel good, to allow you to better understand how your thoughts can work for you, not against you.

When you allow yourself to align to what you want and get specific about it and can feel it and see it and live it in your mind's eye you allow yourself to become a match for it, to manifest it. And in that space, from that realm all of the people, opportunities, situations and circumstances will come to you to allow you to level up.

From that mind-set, with that momentum behind you, suddenly you become aware that even the so called negative things that happen are lessons and opportunities to grow and learn.

Even since I have been coaching and teaching some horrible things have happened to me, I have lost my dad, both my in laws have died, I have lived through a shooting in the Muslim community in Christchurch, there has been a measles outbreak at my girls school, we have lived through a covid impacted world where I was separated entirely from my family for years to asking my husband if we could go home to the UK and him point blank refusing and telling me if I go I go without him. Before doing this work that would have floored me and sent me spiralling downwards to the pit of despair I used to reside in.

But because I understand how personal development and mindset works I understand the control that I have, the choice, and it is always a choice, to either be drawn down into it or rise from it and learn from it.

Bad things happen to all of us but it's the power you attach to them that matters. So I ask you this - do you choose to let your life and your present experience control you or is it time to take your control back and choose a different path, choose to feel a different way, choose to do the work and listen to your inner guidance that has been with you all along trying to get your attention. Everything that you've learned from reading this book, all of the techniques and take away tasks, are designed to put you in momentum towards what you want.

But there is a final warning here, if you have been reading my words and feeling my energy but haven't completed the take away tasks and actually done the work that's not good enough to gain momentum.

You may be feeling inspired, gaining knowledge, feeling uplifted, knowing that there is a better way, that you have a choice BUT although that has the capacity to definitely take you up the emotional guidance scale but it's not enough to get the momentum going. That is exactly why so many people read books and take courses but their life doesn't actually change. Gaining momentum is everything.

So go back now, re-read this book, do the tasks, complete everything and use the emotional guidance scale as a measure of where you are on any given day, of what you feel in the moment. By doing that you will see which practices you enjoy and which ones feel like work.

Focus all of your attention on one the things that excite and inspire you. Use your imagination to take you out of your current situation and place yourself into what you want instead.

Take Away Task

I want you to check in with yourself and be completely real about what take away tasks you have completed and those you haven't.

Don't move on from this book, from these teachings until you've got your own momentum happening.

Use my facebook group, join me, ask questions, in there you have personal access to me, I can coach you through your pain points.

And alternatively if you've done the work you should feel excited and inspired about what comes next. And be thankful, feel gratitude for the lessons you have gained from picking up this book and reading my words.

Really look at where these practices have made a positive impact in your life. So take stock of what you've learned here and start to compartmentalise which tasks you will stick with forever because they made you feel so amazing and which ones felt like work to you, if they felt hard or uninspiring don't do them, never do a task that takes you out of alignment, remember it is all about the way they make you feel, that's the magic.

Your daily affirmations can change your inner dialogue.

Your daily gratitude gives you immediate magic and opens up a world where things are already pretty amazing right here, right now.

Dream day journaling uses your imagination and all of your senses. It connects you directly to what you want.

Your emotional guidance scale shows you how to read your own gauge, to see what you are feeling in any given moment.

Decluttering your mind and your space feeds your momentum because it's something you can physically see as well as emotionally feel.

Meditation connects you to your inner guidance and allows you to truly come back to you after all of these years, that's powerful.

Breathe work calms your mind and your body and aligns you internally to better thoughts and feelings.

Learning to love yourself and create a self-love practice is more powerful and enabling than you could ever know until you do it.

And letting in all of you feelings so that you can heal them and let them go has the potential to heal all of your shadows within your mind and your body, it's phenomenal what a difference that can make.

So I really hope that you can see that all the practices we've been through together are designed specifically to put you into massive growth and momentum, and it's this daily momentum that grows and grows and grows until you naturally focus more on what you do want than what you don't want.

This work makes you fully aware and it's your awareness that has been designed to show you when you're going off track. Where you are heading into critical thoughts, when you are opposing or repelling your desires.

All of these things are powerful and if you bring them into your life it will change, YOU will change.

So again I ask you how badly do you want it. What thoughts do you choose to give your attention to when it comes to changing your life and manifesting what you want moving forward.

End Notes And Thank You's

Before we say goodbye and this book comes to and end I want to thank you for trusting me to start this journey with you. This is only the beginning of your transformation.

Keep this book with you, refer back to it, re-read the words, repeat it over and over until it sinks in and starts to seep unnoticed into your subconscious.

Some of you will have days doing the practices and days off, that's okay. Some of you will let it slide completely and give up, some of you won't even start.

Spiritual growth, in fact any growth isn't about being 100% consistent and disciplined and finding it hard. But if you want something badly enough you need to realize that there is an element of self-encouragement that you need to push yourself on. It's about learning to understand yourself and your patterns and not being hard on yourself if you begin to feel some resistance.

Ask yourself why am I feeling like this? Is this me falling into a self-sabotaging pattern? What is holding me back?

All of this is about understanding yourself. It's about respecting yourself. It's about cheering for yourself.

You've learned so much here but there is always more that can be done. Your life is made up of moments, decisions, beliefs and I encourage you to continue to dream big and do the work that we have started together. Achieving your life from surviving to thriving is all about habits and forming new practices that better serve you in moving forward, not looking back and being hyper critical of yourself.

It's a continual journey to be and do better every day, to be kinder to yourself, to really value yourself.

Surround yourself with positive people and stem the negative flow of things into your life. That may mean that you stop watching the news or mindlessly scrolling social media or why not use social media to your advantage. If you can't surround yourself with positivity in real life do it by following people who light you up, watch amazing YouTube video's and read personal development books such as this one. Make that your priority today and every day of your life moving forward.

It is my hope that what you have learned here, and this really is just the tip of the iceberg, will enable you to spend each day of your life a little bit brighter, a little bit more optimistic, a little bit happier and with a little more self-love.

Lastly but most importantly, remember that you are never, ever alone in your feelings, and that you deserve the world.

And if there is anything else that you need, anything that I can do to help you please do reach out to me.

You can join me in my free facebook community

You can subscribe to my YouTube channel

You can listen to my podcast

Or you can email me at jane@janeelizabeth.online

You can find all of these here – https://linktr.ee/JaneElizabethx

Now go out and live the best life possible, you deserve it.

Love Jane xx

Don't miss out!

Visit the website below and you can sign up to receive emails whenever Jane Adams publishes a new book. There's no charge and no obligation.

https://books2read.com/r/B-A-MPQN-GYOVB

BOOKS 2 READ

Connecting independent readers to independent writers.

About the Author

Hey, I'm Jane x

I am a Mum of two gorgeous girls and a wife to Steve. Prior to having my children I was a careers coach. I then took time out to have my two beautiful girls and started my own business in network marketing. Through this I changed as a person, I delved deeply into personal development and learnt about the law of attraction and my confidence and my perception of myself changed.

My business grew from that passion, mixing the skills and abilities I had from being a careers coach for over fifteen years and the love that I found for self development and the ability to change the way we think and feel.

I specialise in helping people overcome their fears of living a boring life of feeling stuck and mediocre. I am here to allow you to and empower you to live and speak your truth no matter what the negative internal chatter says. My books, programmes and courses will give you the tools and the clarity to change from living in a place of ego and subconscious to one of intuition, trust and consciousness. I will help you to break through the lies holding you back.

I will teach you the importance of understanding your own mind, aligning your thoughts, speaking your truth. Loving yourself first and foremost. Simply put - doing life on your terms and not to please anyone else. All that we desire - the loving relationships, the abundance, the happiness, the choices - it's ALL possible and it all starts within the mind.

Through the modalities I teach AND my own personal journey I have all the tools to support you and together we can create powerful transformational shifts in your world.

I myself have been at the lowest of the low places, learnt how to pick myself up again and move forward to where I am today. I want to pass on my learning experience to help you grow and evolve and change into the person I know you were born to be.

I am here to show you just what's possible when you finally choose yourself.

Love Jane x

.uct-compliance